STUDIES IN HISTORY, ECONOMICS AND PUBLIC LAW

Edited by the
FACULTY OF POLITICAL SCIENCE
OF COLUMBIA UNIVERSITY

Number 219

THE PEACEABLE AMERICANS OF 1860–1861

BY

MARY SCRUGHAM

THE PEACEABLE AMERICANS
OF 1860–1861

A Study in Public Opinion

BY

MARY SCRUGHAM

OCTAGON BOOKS

A DIVISION OF FARRAR, STRAUS AND GIROUX

New York   1976

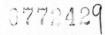

Reprinted 1976
by special arrangement with Columbia University Press

OCTAGON BOOKS
A DIVISION OF FARRAR, STRAUS & GIROUX, INC.
19 Union Square West
New York, N.Y. 10003

Library of Congress Cataloging in Publication Data

Scrugham, Mary, 1885-
    The peaceable Americans of 1860-1861.

    Reprint of the ed. published by Columbia University, New York
as no. 219 of Studies in history, economics and public law.

    Originally presented as the author's thesis, Columbia University,
1921.

    1. United States—History—Civil War, 1861-1865—Causes.
2. United States—Politics and government, 1857-1861. 3. Ken-
tucky—Politics and government—1792-1865. I. Title. II.
Series: Columbia studies in the social sciences; no. 219.
E440.5.S437   1976   973-7'11   70-159252
ISBN 0-374-97208-7

Manufactured by Braun-Brumfield, Inc.
Ann Arbor, Michigan
Printed in the United States of America

To the

GREAT NATIONALIST

HENRY CLAY

WHOSE GENIUS DIVINED AND WHOSE SKILL EFFECTED THE
CONCILIATIONS WHICH WERE ESSENTIAL TO THE
PERPETUATION OF A NATIONAL UNITY BASED
ON THE COMMON CONSENT OF THE
NORTH AND THE SOUTH, THE
EAST AND THE WEST
ALIKE

PREFACE

The title and contents of this monograph have undergone an evolutionary process. In its most rudimentary form, the title was "The Reconstruction Period in Kentucky." When it was ascertained that the reconstruction ardently desired by the Kentuckians was a peaceful, pre-war affair, the title immediately underwent transformation in order to make a distinction between pre-war and post-war reconstruction. In its final form it deals with the pre-war period.

That the Kentuckians of 1861 were the most Constitution-abiding and peaceable of all Americans was not necessarily the result of preëminent ability in the science of government but was chiefly due to their geographical location. They were situated in the center of the nation and were therefore equipped with a better understanding of the governmental problem confronting the nation than would have been possible had they inhabited a region less in touch with the current of opinion in all sections.

Kentucky's decision in 1861 was that neither secession on the part of the South, nor coercion on the part of the North, was a justifiable solution for the governmental problem of the time. The Kentuckians felt that the conditions existing in 1861 did not warrant such extreme measures but did warrant the assembling of a National Convention such as that which met the great crisis at the other critical period in the nation's life with success. They felt that the brain of the American people was capable of adjusting the existing difficulties and therefore strenuously opposed an appeal to arms. The following account is in some measure an explanation of the point of view which caused the peaceable Americans of 1861 to arrive at such a conclusion and to demand the calling of a National Constitutional Convention to settle the dispute.

The completion of this monograph leaves me deeply indebted to the following persons: to Mr. Cabell Bullock, for encouragement at the psychological moment; to Miss Grace Everson for assistance in collecting data; to Dr. Glanville Terrell, for his Grecian readiness to argue indefatigably; and to the late Mrs. Desha Breckinridge, for an inspiring confidence.

There are a number of persons who have assisted in the preparation of this work by making available the data on which it is based. Chief among them are: Mrs. Mary Crittenden Haycraft, Miss Sophonisba Breckinridge, Mr. John Fitzpatrick, Judge Shackelford Miller, Judge George C. Webb, Mr. John Wilson Townsend, Mrs. Thomas H. Clay and Mr. Harrison Simrall.

However, in so far as this historical account is an intellectual achievement of any merit, my heaviest debt of gratitude is to Professor William A. Dunning of Columbia University who rivals Socrates in the subtle art of questioning and to whom, I and many other students of Political Science are profoundly grateful for the teaching of a great master.

ALLENDALE, MARCH 7, 1921.

CONTENTS

CHAPTER I

American Ideas in Regard to the Abolition of Slavery on the Eve of Civil War

Across the Atlantic in 1861, philosophers and statesmen asked one another why twenty-five million intelligent Americans could not settle the condition of four million uneducated Africans without tearing one another's throats. Doubtless some thought with Alexander H. Stephens of Georgia, that the Americans lacked both sense and patriotism. Lord Bryce has reached the conclusion that fighting could have been averted had our governmental organization been equipped with a cabinet system such as the English then had. However, Mr. James Ford Rhodes and other authoritative historians have decided that a blood-letting conflict was really inevitable in America, because the North believed that slavery was wrong and the South believed that slavery was right and they thus unalterably expressed themselves at the presidential election of November 6, 1860.

Nevertheless, in reading through the files of newspapers and letters bearing the date, 1860, one is deeply impressed with the fact that the Americans as a people no more foresaw and willed the event which was about to transpire in 1861 than the Belgian people in 1913 foresaw and willed the war which was so soon to break upon them. Certainly the political platforms on which the candidates stood in the presidential campaign of 1860 contained no planks with clear-cut policies in regard to the coming event which the election of 1860 is supposed to have unalterably determined. The platform most pleasing to the cotton-growing slave states contained no ultimatum to the northern free states in regard to slavery. The platform on which Lincoln stood merely asserted that the southern demand for the protection of slavery in the national territories by the national government, on the ground that the Supreme Court had declared that slaves were property, should not be granted. The platform emphatically opposed the extension of slavery into the national territories under the auspices of the federal government and declared in favor of the national government's prohibiting extension of slavery into the territories. Thus the Republican platform is a far cry from an explicit declaration in favor of a bloody emancipation of the slaves in the southern slave states. It is miles away from a declaration in favor of emancipation without compensation to the owner.

The slaves themselves were quite unaware that a blood and iron emancipation was impending and on the whole were unconscious of a desire for it. The free white labor which existed side by side with slave labor in the southern states signally failed to realize the irrepressibleness of the conflict between the two systems and voted almost unanimously against the candidate who prophesied the " all free eventually " system and who advocated the prohibition of slavery in the national territories. Nor did the free white laborers of the North feel called upon to vote overwhelmingly for free soil, much less did they express a desire to lay down their lives to bring freedom to the negro slaves of the South. One of the spokesmen of the northern labor organizations declared against negro emancipation on the ground that the blacks would be economically in a worse position under the system of wage labor than they were under slavery: for the " poor negro leads the life of a farm horse; the poor white that of

a horse kept at a livery stable who is worked by everybody
and cared for by nobody." [1]

In view of the prevalence of such indifferent ideas in regard to abolition in 1860, there seemed no prospect for the
" irrepressible conflict " to burst into flame the following year.
There was no intimation on the part of the American people
that they had any serious plans for undertaking to free the
Africans at all. The leading issue in the presidential campaign concerning the negro was solely, in the North, that
of excluding him by law from the national territories from
which he had already been excluded by economic facts,[2] inasmuch as the soil and climate of the national territories
were such as to render the growing of cotton, sugar and
tobacco unprofitable, even if there had been enough negroes
in the country to establish the system in more new territories. The Republican platform proposed to make assurance doubly sure by prohibiting slaves in the national
territories by statute law in order to satisfy that portion of
the northern mind which did not comprehend the significance of economic facts; and in order to ease the consciences
of those who were troubled over their joint responsibility
for human slavery in regions under national and not state
control; and last but not least perhaps, in order to gratify
the Republican party politicians' inextinguishable ambition
for public office.

Who then willed that the " irrepressible conflict " [3] should
begin in 1861 ? Absolutely, there is no evidence that the

---

[1] George H. Evans in Working Men's Advocate. Quoted in Schlü-
ter's Lincoln, Labor and Slavery.

[2] Rhodes, vol. ii, p. 418. " Nowhere in the existing territory of the
country was there the possibility of carving out another slave state."

[3] The phrase " irrepressible conflict " as understood by the mass of
northern people during the pre-war period did not signify an armed
conflict.

American people, when they gave their votes at the polls on November 6, 1860, expressed themselves in favor of fighting as the method of their choice for settling the condition of four million uneducated Africans.

However, coming events usually cast their shadows before them. Bad blood existed between the spokesmen of some of the northern states and some of the southern states. It had arisen in the course of arguments in the national Congress over the benefits and disadvantages of the slave labor system. The one set exaggerated the evil and the other, the good of the slave labor system, so that the "heaven they argued no nearer to them got, but gave them a taste for something a thousand times as hot." The result of these heated debates at Washington was that the statements of the extremists in the North and in the South came to be regarded in the opposite section as a fair sample of the views of the masses of people in the section whence the representative who had uttered them originated.

In addition to the practice of this bad logic both in the North and in the South in regard to the numbers of persons who entertained extreme views on either side of the slavery question, a tendency existed in the South to make no discrimination between the anti-slavery policies advocated by Garrison, Brown, Seward and Lincoln, respectively. To many a southerner these northerners were all abolitionists of the same hue. Southern newspapers and politicians used the words " abolitionist " and " Republican " as synonyms.[1] There was, of course, some ground for this confusion after 1858. Lincoln's house-divided-against-itself-cannot-stand speech made in that year sanctioned the abolitionist ideal, though he advocated no program at that time to bring about its realization other than the prohibition

[1] Sherman papers, William T. Sherman to John Sherman, Oct. 3, 1860.

of slavery in the territories.   Seward took practically the
same stand in a more vigorous speech at Rochester, N. Y.,
a few months after Lincoln had ventured to open up this
new political prospect of " all free eventually " as a goal
for the Republican party.   It was in this speech that
Seward asserted that an irrepressible conflict existed between slave and free labor and Lincoln concurred in this
phrasing of the matter on the eve of his nomination for the
presidency by the Republican party.   In 1859, John Brown
made an attempt to bring about the freedom of the negroes
by a raid into Virginia in the hope of inciting the slaves to
an insurrection which would result in their own emancipation.   Garrison, the founder of the " Liberator," a paper
devoted to preaching the gospel of freedom for everybody,
was as much opposed to the use of violence as a method of
liberating the African as he was to slavery itself.   He was
a moral-suasionst.   However, the southerners made no
careful distinctions between politicians, direct actionists and
moral-suasionists.   If the majority of southerners ever
knew that the Republican platform on which Lincoln and
Seward stood denounced John Brown's raid into Virginia
as an infamous crime and gave only a ray of hope to
Garrison, they doubtless considered it subtle hypocrisy.[1]

[1] The following resolutions adopted by the Democrats of Tennessee
will serve to illustrate southern feeling toward the Republicans:

  Resolved: That the organization of the Republican party upon
strictly sectional principles, and its hostility to the institution of
slavery, which is recognized by the Constitution, and which is in-
separably connected with the social and industrial pursuits of the
southern states of the confederacy, is war upon the principles of
the Constitution and upon the rights of the states.

  Resolved: That the late treasonable invasion of Virginia by a
band of Republicans was the necessary result of the doctrines and
teachings of that party; was the beginning of the " irrepressible
conflict " of Mr. Seward; was a blow aimed at the institution of
slavery by an effort to excite servile insurrection.

  Official Proceedings of the Democratic Convention, p. 69.

The inhabitants of the border free and border slave states had a much better opportunity to become acquainted with the distinctions which the various leaders of opinion made in regard to slavery. It was undoubtedly clear to most of the border states people that a majority of the northern people, when they thought about it at all, may have hoped that slavery would eventually be abolished in a way perfectly satisfactory to the southern people.[1]   But the subject did not greatly concern the mass of northerners except when it was thrust upon their attention by a runaway negro, a pathetic story, or a radical press.   The great mass of northern people gave no evidence of feeling such an intense and sustained sympathy with the southern slaves and such a bitter antipathy to the system that they would be willing to tax themselves to accomplish the freeing of the negroes by purchase or that they would be willing to lay down their lives in a crusade to free them at the point of a bayonet.   Toward immediate emancipation the attitude of the vast majority of northern people was one of blank indifference.   Comparatively, Gerrit Smiths and John Browns were very rare, but their numbers appeared all too plentiful to the South, where John Brownism on its reverse side of servile insurrection came to the fireside of every southern home.   Slaveholder and non-slaveholder were unanimously opposed to encouraging the slaves to murder their masters and their masters' families or whoever happened to get in their way.

[1] The following quotation from the *Louisville Journal*, Aug. 14, 1860, shows the border-state point of view: " We seriously believe that when the North and the South meet each other face to face and eye to eye: when they take their ideas of each other's sentiments and opinions from unprejudiced sources, and not through the perverted mediums of stump speeches, partisan diatribes, buncombe resolutions, they will be prepared to fraternize most cordially, and kick parties, politicians, platforms and schemers into the pit of Tophet."

Though the methods of Lincoln and Brown were different, their aims were identical. They both heartily hated the southern domestic institution of slavery and desired its abolition.[1] Lincoln possessed political sagacity to a high degree and well understood the force of public opinion. He realized that violence on behalf of a reform produced *per se* in the public mind a reaction against the reform. He felt that it was useless to run too far ahead of public opinion in attempting to bring about the emancipation of the slaves. Therefore he aimed to go only so far and so fast as public opinion would sustain him at each step—that is to say just far enough to lead, just a little way ahead. Brown, on the other hand, had no practical sagacity of this variety. He thought that public opinion could be accelerated by direct action and was willing to lay down his own life to advertise the wrong of slavery, though the effect he desired his death to produce was somewhat dimmed by the numbers of women and children, slave-holder and non-slaveholder, who would meet death were his methods successful. Most people find difficulty in believing that it is consistent " to inaugurate the principles of heaven with the artillery of hell." The cure is worse than the disease.

When Lincoln sounded the " eventually all free " note in his campaign against Douglas, he had a very definite political object in view. His immediate purpose was to win enough votes to get elected to the United States Senate. His ground for asking for the votes of his fellow Illinois citizens was that he would represent those who did not want slavery to spread into any of the national territories. He promised to vote to prevent the extension of slavery should he be successful in winning the election. However, at the time he was making this race for the Senate with Douglas, it was becoming increasingly clear that slavery did not have

---

[1] Lincoln said he hated slavery as much as any abolitionist.

the ghost of a show for establishment in any of the unsettled lands then belonging to the nation because the economic basis for the system was lacking in all of them. The defeat of the slave-state constitution in Kansas made it certain that none of the land which Douglas had opened to slavery north of 36° 30′ would become slave. In view of the economic circumstances it was becoming more and more evident that unless the Republican party acquired new tenets there was no reason for continuing its organization. The purpose for which it had been organized, i. e., restoring the free status of the land lying north of 36° 30′, having been accomplished, it would fall to pieces unless it acquired other reasons to continue its existence. Seward, one of the leading lights of the party, and Greeley, the leading editor of the party, were willing at this time to dissolve the party, but Lincoln was unwilling for the Republicans to disband their distinctive anti-slavery organization and have nobody to follow but Douglas,[1] who did not care whether slavery was " voted up or voted down." Accordingly, in his debate with Douglas, he had to supply additional material for the sustenance of the party's life; for the time was rapidly approaching when it would become obvious to everybody that the extension of slavery into the territories had been checked permanently by prevailing economic conditions. In order to win victory at the polls in 1858 it would be necessary for a Republican candidate not only to hold persons already enrolled in the moribund political organization, but also to gain additional recruits to the cause of prohibition of slavery in the territor-

---

[1] Rhodes, vol. ii, p. 329. Lincoln said " [Douglas's] hope rested on the idea of visiting the great ' Black Republican ' Party and making it the tail of his new kite. He knows he was then expecting from day to day to turn Republican and place himself at the head of our organization." Also see p. 308.

ies by federal law. The two groups from which new
members could be drawn were the bona-fide abolitionists
and the Henry Clay " Whigs " who had hitherto refused
to enroll themselves in a sectional political party. · The
abolitionists supplied the soul of the anti-slavery movement
of the North, but they in general had refused to vote for
anybody who compromised on anything less than a declaration in favor of abolition of slavery in the slave states. The
Henry Clay Whigs of the North opposed a further acquisi-
tion of territory which could be devoted to slavery but desired ultimate abolition only under conditions equitable to
the South. They had the most kindly feelings toward the
southern whites and like Clay they preferred the liberty of
their own race to that of any other race, although they were
no friends of slavery.

Lincoln so skillfully calculated the wording of his famous
House-Divided speech that it won converts to his following
from both of the above mentioned groups. It carried water
on both shoulders, so to speak, for it was so constructed
that it was acceptable to both radicals and moderate conservatives. The first part of the paragraph which follows
contained bait for abolitionist consumption:

A house divided against itself cannot stand. I believe this government cannot endure permanently half slave and half free. I
do not expect the Union to be dissolved, but I do expect it will
cease to be divided. It will become all one thing or all the other.
Either the opponents of slavery will arrest the further spread of
it, and place it where the public mind shall rest in the belief that
it is in the course of ultimate extinction, or its advocates will push
it forward till it shall become alike lawful in all the States, old
as well as new, North as well as South.

The last part of this paragraph veils the radicalism of the
first part of it and makes of the whole what many Henry
Clay Whigs even in the South hoped. The idea presented

in the above quoted paragraph to the effect that the advocates of slavery intended to push slavery forward into the
northern states unless the system was checked and put on its
way to ultimate extinction contained a powerful cement for
amalgamating the heterogeneous elements of the North into
one sectional party opposed to such extension. It was a
trumpet call to the North to form into solid cohorts to prevent such aggression on their rights. Lincoln, it is recorded,
gave a great deal of thought to the construction of that
paragraph. It carried in it the future destiny of the Republican party. By that paragraph the masterful leader
gently cut the party loose from its old Whig moorings and
warily charted its course to the port of the abolitionists. It
was really an epoch-making utterance. Its meaning and importance depended on the various interpretations that would
and could be given it in different parts of the country.[1]

As we all know Douglas defeated Lincoln in the sena-
torial election, but Lincoln saved the life of the Republican
party by his timely and revivifying remarks. The defeat
merely indicated to the consolidator of northern opinion
that public opinion was not yet ready to approve the unsailed
course which led to the port of the abolitionists, the goal he
had provided for his party in the House-Divided speech.
For the present it was sufficiently nourishing to the party's

[1] Sherman papers, T. Webster to John Sherman, Nov. 15, 1860. An
interview with Lincoln is recounted in this letter, which shows the
variation of meaning possible by mere emphasis. "He (Lincoln) met
some Kentuckians in the afternoon. They said that they had great
difficulty to explain away his speech at Springfield, two years ago, to
the effect that a house divided against itself cannot stand. He laughed
and proceeded to quote it, laying no stress on the words 'permanently
endure.' He asked the Kentuckians if that was not their opinion. Of
course they replied, 'Yes.' 'Then,' said he, 'if you may so express
yourselves, why may not I?' All present laughed, 'Old Abe' the
loudest of all. He left the Kentuckians under the impression that it
would occur some day but in the day of a future generation."

life to have "all free" enshrined as an ultimate ideal and
to spread the idea that the South would be satisfied with
nothing less than "all slave."

The interpretation which the House-Divided speech received during the presidential campaign of 1860 varied with
latitude and longitude. In conservative New York it received the emphasis appropriate for attracting the conservative. In ultra-conservative districts and in the border
slave states it was sought to have it taken in connection with
all the conservative remarks that its author had ever made.
In the abolitionist stronghold of the Western Reserve the
first sentences of the "all free eventually" paragraph were
strongly featured, thus gaining abolitionist support for the
candidate. It was these same sentences which received
emphasis in the slave states. These astute sentences were
provocative of intense distrust of their author throughout the
entire slave-holding section. They of the South had the
feeling that it encouraged John Brownism.[1] The John
Brown raid had occurred in the interim between the speech
and the nomination for the presidency which Lincoln won
from his party largely because of this House-Divided
speech. It was less radical than Seward's "Irrepressible
Conflict" and yet it was not essentially conservative.
Many southerners were fully prepared to expect a series
of John Brown raids or a big John Brown raid into the
South in the event of the succession of Lincoln to the
administration of the national government. They were all
more or less ready to become convinced that the opening

[1] See John C. Breckenridge's statement in the address to the Kentucky Legislature, Dec., 1859. "Though I am far from asserting that
the mass of the Republican party contemplated such atrocious proceedings in Virginia, yet I assert, with a profound conviction of the truth,
my belief that the horrible tragedy is but the forerunner of a blazing
border war, unless the spirit they are fomenting in this land can be
arrested by a general outbreak of conservative opinion."

of " the irrepressible conflict " which the Republicans believed in would be inaugurated soon after the Black Republicans or abolitionists came into control of the federal government. The destruction of the domestic tranquility of the South was imminent. They felt that their constitutional rights were infringed by the election of a president by northern votes to preside over southern welfare. Lincoln was more than *persona non grata* to the most intelligent classes of the South. To them he was a " dangerous man." The more astute judged him to be the " northern arrow of radical fanaticism winged with conservatism." [1]

In view of the interpretation placed on the House-Divided speech in the South and the blending of it with what John Brown had done and Seward prophesied, it should hardly be a matter of surprise that the presidental candidate who represented such an ensemble of possibilities for the South did not receive a single vote in ten of the slave states and had relatively very few in the others, which were border slave states and thus had a better opportunity to discriminate between the varieties of northern opinion. As a matter of fact, the wealth of a Rothschild could not have bought an electoral vote for Lincoln in any of the slave states.

Such were the ideas current in the United States in regard to the abolition of slavery on the eve of the outbreak of the Civil War which has been regarded as an " irrepressible conflict." It is especially significant to note the ideas prevalent in the South regarding what ideas were prevalent in the North and to realize that it is not things as they are which are important in the political life of a Republic but things as they seem or can be made to seem.

[1] *Louisville Journal*, May 19, 1860.

CHAPTER II

THE NATIONALISTIC BASIS OF NEUTRALITY

Two-fifths of the American people voting on November 6, 1860, voted for electors pledged to vote for Abraham Lincoln as President of the United States and three-fifths of them voted for electors pledged to vote against him. Of those who voted against him, less than one-fifth voted for the Breckinridge electors favoring federal protection of slavery in the national territories. The remainder of those voting against Lincoln equaled over two-fifths of the total vote and constituted a plurality. It is very important to note that this plurality voted neither for the anti-slavery candidate nor for the pro-slavery candidate. It registered itself neutral between Lincoln on the northern side and Breckinridge on the southern side.

The basis of this neutrality was a desire for a peaceful perpetuation of the Union. The neutrals believed that the control of the national government by a sectional party such as that of Lincoln or Breckinridge was thoroughly inconsistent with the principle that government derives its just powers from the consent of the governed. They apparently felt that "consent" necessarily should be common to the American people, common in the sense that the Common Law was common to all the regions of England. If a sectional or geographical party gained control of the national administration—no matter on what issue—government based on consent of the governed would be abrogated for the geographical region which furnished no membership in the administration party. If the general government promoted the interests of one section of the country regardless of the welfare of the whole it was to be feared, as Henry Clay had so clearly shown, that the section, or sections, whose vital interests were neglected would seek a government which would afford requisite consideration. For a great outcry would at once arise in the section totally unrepresented in the administration to the effect that " The North shall rule the North " or the " South shall rule the South," as the case happened to be. The neutrals believed that the true standard was represented by the motto, " Americans shall rule America " and not by " Northerners shall rule America " or by " Southerners shall rule the whole land." Only a policy which was the greatest common divisor, so to speak, of the interests of every section should be the policy administered at Washington. That which was common to the interests and wishes of the whole nation was national; *that which was peculiar to one section was sectional.* Obviously, any policy of one section which was abhorrent to the interests of another section was essentially sectional in character.

Over two-fifths of the American people opposed the formation of political parties championing respectively the sectional policies of the North and the South in regard to free and slave labor. Such political parties would necessarily draw their entire membership from opposite geographical areas—one from the North exclusively and the other from the South largely. The parting injunction of Washington to his countrymen contained a solemn warning against the formation of geographical political parties because he felt that such parties would endanger the very existence of the Union. The nationalistic party policy earnestly recommended by Washington was strictly followed by the neutrals of 1860, but was entirely disregarded by the Republicans.

However, the Republicans maintained that they were not violating Washington's solemn injunction. According to Republican logic, the fact that everybody in every section of the country had the privilege of voting in favor of the Republican candidates made the Republican party national and entirely eliminated its purely geographical character— even though it was well understood that the inhabitants of the southern section would refrain with unparalleled unanimity from voting for the northern sectional candidates.[1] The neutrals of 1860 asserted that a sectionalized treatment of the slavery question would produce a geographical " line up" that would result in a " fast gallop to perdition."

The plurality regarded an " irrepressible conflict " between the slave and free labor systems as the " mere nonsensical vagary of Lincoln and Seward with which they exposed their very small pretensions to philosophical statesmanship." For the plurality considered Lincoln's application of the House-Divided-Against-Itself parable to the labor question as contradictory of fact. The Union based on consent had stood from 1776 to 1860 sustained partly by the toil of free and partly by the toil of slave labor. It had grown great and prospered thus constituted. And if such a conflict was brewing during the twenty-five years previous to 1860 it was precisely the epoch of " unprecedented prosperity to both the North and the South." The foundation and preservation of the Union were not the outcome of harping on the differences of opinion and interests among the states but were the result of the emphasis which its

---

[1] See Lincoln in Cooper Union speech. " You say we are sectional. We deny it. We get no votes in your section. The fact is substantially true. . . . Some of you delight to flaunt in our faces the warning against sectional parties given by Washington in his Farewell Address. . . . We respect that warning of Washington, and we commend it to you, together with his example, pointing to the right application of it."

founders and preservers had continually placed on the common purposes of the various sections. Solely by this emphasis on compatibilities and on common interests had the thirteen original states and their territories been welded into a nation. If this policy were abandoned for Lincoln's, the kingbolt of the great Union based on consent would be shattered and this species of Union could not long survive without it. For a sectional minority to undo the mighty and magnificent work of Washington and Madison, of Clay and Webster, was traitorous to the Union because it was a violation of the essential principle which had made and preserved the United States a nation from 1776 to 1860. For a sectional minority administration at Washington to propagate exclusively a sectional standard unacceptable and hostile to another section and thereby to forsake the national mean for the sectional extreme, was the greatest possible of political vices under a government which derives its just powers from the consent of the governed; for, if a sectional minority put into national effect its own peculiar sectional policy, it would be destructive to the cardinal principle of American Government for the non-concurring sections.

In the electoral colleges the holders of the above doctrines did not win a plurality, much less a majority of the votes, because under the actual working of our presidential electoral system, the registering of the neutrals' voting strength was dissipated. The neutrals were handicapped by being divided into two groups. One of these groups was under the leadership of Stephen A. Douglas and the other under that of John Bell.

Douglas explained the basis of his position very thoroughly in the Lincoln-Douglas debates of 1858.[1] He cham-

[1] Rhodes, ii, pp. 318, 319. See also, typical speech of Douglas in Fite's *Presidential Campaign of 1860*, pp. 227-300. And also, a speech by A. H. Stephens in support of Douglas, *Louisville Democrat*, Sept. 16, 1860.

pioned the great principle of self-determination not only for states but also for territories. The best way to settle the territorial labor question which was constantly causing dissension whenever its settlement was discussed in Congress, was to let the people who actually inhabited the territory settle the question for themselves in their territorial legislatures. He asserted that the adoption of this method would " secure peace, harmony and good-will " among the sections by removing the controversy from the halls of Congress to the western plains. Douglas announced that he was neither for nor against slavery. It was immaterial to him whether slavery was " voted up or voted down." He had incorporated the great principle of self-determination for the peoples of the territories in the Kansas-Nebraska Bill. Since Kansas had adopted a free-state constitution he stood squarely for admitting Kansas as a free state. It was entirely up to the people of the territory to decide the question for themselves. This policy of self-determination (or " squatter sovereignty " or " popular sovereignty " as it was then called) Douglas held to be perfectly just to every section of the nation and, therefore, thoroughly fit to be adopted as a national policy in regard to slavery in the territories.

It will be remembered that the Kansas-Nebraska Bill of which Douglas was the author, repealed an earlier agreement between the representatives of the North and the South for the exclusion of slavery from land lying north of the parallel 36° 30'. The enactment of Douglas's Kansas-Nebraska measure had two major effects.

First. It gave the southern slave-state politicians a chance to manufacture another slave state and to bring two more Senators into the United States Senate from a state not hostile to the slave labor system. Up to 1850 there had been an equal number of free and slave states. By 1860 the balance had been destroyed. There were then 18 free and 15 slave states; thus there were six more senators from free than from slave states. Nobody understood any better than Jefferson Davis and the other southern representatives what the steadily increasing free-state majority meant. They realized that no more slave territories meant no more slave states and that no more slave states meant that the balance in the Senate was hopelessly upset and that the southern senators would be utterly powerless to check hostile legislation by the veto of the Senate as formerly. Therefore, self-determination for the slave states themselves was thus in danger. However, the Kansas-Nebraska measure failed to produce the result so much desired by the southerners who helped Douglas to pass it—even though the most desperate efforts were made by the southerners, abetted by President Buchanan, to nullify the will of the Kansans and bring Kansas in as a slave state whether or no. Douglas denounced this as a fraud and prevented its consummation. He, himself, was in turn denounced by Buchanan and the southerners as recreant to principle and as faithless to the trusts of friendship. Douglas felt unable to renounce the great principle of self-determinaton for the territories to save the slave-state balance in the Senate. Douglas was applauded for his stand by his constituents in the North and also he retained a numerous following in the southern slave states. This action of Douglas in regard to the admission of Kansas led to the formation of an ultra pro-slavery party which demanded federal protection for slave property in the territories. The southerners were led to demand every iota of their constitutional property rights, since they saw that it would require a good deal more than self-determination for the territories to produce any more slave states. They came to look upon Douglas's doctrine of self-determination in the territories as but another name for free-soilism.. Thus, Douglas, the nationalist, was indirectly responsible for the formation of a southern sectional party whose purpose was to propagate slavery in the territories to keep the balance in the Senate from becoming ultimately too heavily weighted against the slave states.

Second. The other great result of the Kansas-Nebraska measure was to call into existence a free-state party to prevent the spread of slavery into territories already consecrated to freedom by the agreement made at the time Missouri was admitted to the Union. Thus, Douglas, the nationalist, was also responsible for the formation of a northern sectional party. The immediate reason for organizing this party of which Lincoln was the presidential candidate in 1860, was to restore the free status of the territory north of 36° 30' opened to slavery by the astute Douglas through the passage of the Kansas-Nebraska measure granting self-determination to the territories. By 1858 dimly and by 1860 clearly, it was evident that in spite of the legal chance offered in the Kansas-Nebraska measure not a foot of the territory would become slave. Economic facts were a more certain prohibition than law. Climate and soil had closed the western territories forever to slavery. When it became clear that the great purpose for the existence of the Republican party had been accomplished with the death of slavery in Kansas, the Republican party leaders looked around for other reasons to to justify their continuation as an organization. As has been related in the first chapter, Seward and Greeley had been willing to renounce their sectional political organization, but Lincoln had intervened and had supplied additional material for party purposes by the goal he held up in the House-Divided speech in 1858. Douglas charged Lincoln with coming out on behalf of the Republican party in favor of uniformity of domestic institutions in the slave and free states and with continuing the sectional agitation to the place where it would end in sectional warfare. Lincoln sharply replied to the effect that the present slavery agitation which Douglas professed a desire to settle peacefully was of Douglas's own rousing. Had it not been for Douglas's attempt to give the slave-owners another slave state made from territory already consecrated to freedom there would be no agitation. He said that Douglas and not Lincoln was responsible for rousing the dormant anti-slavery opinion in the North, which had hitherto been satisfied that the system was on its way to ultimate extinction. He pointed to "bleeding Kansas," where the pro-slavery and the anti-slavery settlers had battled for control of the state constitutional convention, as a sample of the peace which Douglas's scheme produced.

Charge and counter charge were made as to the section which was responsible for the then heated controversy over slavery in the territories. We are reminded of the recriminations of a family row destined for the divorce court for settlement. Who began the quarrel is always regarded of great importance. But it is not necessarily the only important point to be considered. Starting the ball a-rolling is never an adequate reason for not accounting the person who did the starting sincere in wanting it to stop before it entirely smashes up domestic tranquility, or any excuse for the second party to the quarrel giving the ball a vigorous kick when the momentum from the original push is becoming exhausted.

So much for the Douglas type of neutrality. The other group of nationalistic neutrals entered the campaign of 1860 under the caption of Constitutional Unionists and were led by John Bell.[1] They were guiltless of fomenting sectional

[1] The columns of the *Louisville Journal*, the leading Bell paper, are authoritative for this party's program.

agitation in " any shape or form." They desired to check
" Disunionism in the South and prostrate Abolition fanaticism in the North." They belonged to the school of Henry
Clay, the great nationalist. These old-line Whigs had af-
filiated with neither the Republican nor the Democratic organization since the break-up of the former Whig party.
Great numbers of them had voted the Know-Nothing or
Native American ticket in 1856. The Know-Nothings
were chiefly opposed to the exercise of so large an influence
in American affairs by foreign-born persons and Catholics.
They wished to stiffen the requirements for American
citizenship. With the break-up of the Know-Nothing
movement after its failure to make any impression on the
policy of the government, both Republicans and Democrats
made overtures to the politically unattached. Lincoln, himself, had once been a Henry Clay Whig and the Republicans
attracted into their fold large numbers of the former Whigs
on the ground that the Republicans' program had been advocated by Henry Clay. And all through the campaign of
1860, the Republicans systematically claimed Clay and held
out Douglas's anti-Clayism for inspection. However, the
Clay Whigs, especially of the South, perceived a difference
between old Whiggery and Republicanism. George D.
Prentice, editor of the *Louisville Journal,* and a life-long
friend and disciple of Clay, explained the difference as follows:

There is not a Black Republican spot or blot on the shining
public record of Henry Clay. Not one. Not a shadow of one.
No, the difference between the position of Mr. Clay and that of
the Republican party is manifest and irreconcilable. It is the
difference between the Compromise of 1850 and the Wilmot Pro-
viso, between the national mean and the sectional extreme, between
peace and amity and unity on the one hand and discord and
revenge and dissolution on the other. The difference is broad,
distinct and undeniable. It is vital. It is glaring. It can be

neither erased nor obscured. There it is and all the floods of fanaticism cannot wash it out, nor all the webs of sophistry disguise it.[1]

The southern neutrals numbered in their ranks many of the large slave-owners, who were opposed to a dissolution of the Union and the tactics of the extreme States Rights school. They were inclined to think that there was, indeed, an " irrepressible conflict " but that it was a conflict between politicians and that it was likely to continue as long as the people of the two sections permitted their prejudices to be played upon for party benefit. As to an " irrepressible conflict " between free and slave labor which was nationally injurious, they considered the announcement of such a conflict " about the grossest falsehood that ever was palmed on a gullible nation " and that the whole national experience was " its complete disproof." Lincoln looked upon these southern unionists as " white crows." [2]

For all practical purposes the Constitutional Unionists were at one with the Douglas Democrats on the territorial slavery issue of 1860.[3] They were neither pro-slavery nor anti-slavery for the territories then in the possession of the nation. Whereas, the southern Democrats (and a corporal's guard of northern Democrats under the leadership of Buchanan) favored wielding the powers of the national government for the extension of slavery in the territories, and the Republicans considered this utterly wrong and favored the use of those powers for just the opposite purpose, the Constitutional Unionists proposed to do neither. They were neutral, though they recognized the right of the Supreme Court to adjudicate the legal questions involved in the territorial slavery question. But they pointed out that

[1] *Louisville Journal*, April 26. 1860.
[2] Weed's *Weed*, vol. i, p. 606.
[3] *Louisville Journal*, April 13, 1860, Oct. 31, 1860, and *passim*.

there was no territory in 1860 to which slavery could be profitably taken. They considered it madness to rave about imaginary territory, when slavery could hardly occupy the territory it already had. Since no southern planter was deprived of his emigrating privileges, and no northern man was deprived of any free soil, the territorial question was already settled. It had settled itself. They felt that the whole territorial slavery question which was the ostensible cause of the sectional agitation and the sectional bitterness, was a mere abstraction.

However, it was no easy task for the neutrals of 1860 to fight shoulder to shoulder in the campaign of 1860. The Democratic and Whig contingents were ancient enemies.[1] The Whigs in general, even many southern Whigs, had opposed the passage of the Kansas-Nebraska measure. They saw in the author of this bill, Stephen A. Douglas, the immediate cause of the great wave of sectionalism which they sought to check before it wrecked the Union. " Why," the Constitutional Unionists asked, " did Douglas unsettle the Compromise? " " For the love of the Union, eh? He tells us that he pledged himself to Henry Clay at his death bed, that he would be true to the dying statesman's Compromise of 1850. . . . What is the Douglas Union panacea? To unsettle every peaceful adjustment. This is the sweet milk of concord with a vengeance." [2]

[1] See James O. Harrison's account in his unprinted sketches of public men, pp. 59-60. " They (the mass of men) could not be aroused to the imminence of the danger. Even conservative men of other political organizations would not lay aside for the time their differences on minor questions, and therefore they would not unite with the Democrats against the common enemy of them all. They would shrug their shoulders and say with the utmost complacency that they had never given a Democratic vote, and that should the struggle come, it would merely be a struggle . . . for political supremacy. . . ."

[2] *Louisville Journal*, July 11, 1860.

An additional reason for the neutrals' inability to do perfect team work in the face of the common danger, was the
Know-Nothing record of the Constitutional Unionists.
The Democrats, especially the northern Democrats, had wel-
comed the foreign born into full political fellowship and
even shared with them the spoils of office. The memory of
the recent contest on the native American issue was still
green and the Republican politicians and editors who hoped
to turn the election in some places with the German vote,
took care to refresh the memories of any who perchance had
forgotten.

Nevertheless, in spite of ancient prejudices and differences of opinion, a partial fusion of the nationalistic
neutrals took place before the campaign of 1860 was well
under way.[1] Their common ground was a peaceful preservation of the Union with the national government under
national control. They continually reminded the American
people of the prophetic warnings of Washington against
sectional or geographical parties and called upon the
American people to lay aside their customary party predilec-
tions " as a sacrifice on the altar of their country." The
leaders of both groups, especially the southerners, fully ap-
preciated the prospect before the nation in the event of a
purely sectional party's gaining control of the national government. They keenly felt that such an unwise experiment
in the perpetuation of the Union should not be made.
These lovers of the Union were dubbed " Union-savers "
in derision by both the Lincoln and the Breckinridge fac-

---

[1] Bell papers, A. H. H. Stuart to Bell, August 23, 1860; August Bel-
mont to Bell, Aug. 9, 1860; Washington Hunt to Bell, Nov. 21, 1860.
Practically all of the newspapers of the period bear witness to the
fusion movement. The coalition was more thorough in some states than
others. For instance, the *Yeoman* (Ky.), Sept. 20, 1860, states that
" Billing and cooing takes place upon every stump in Kentucky between
the Bell and Douglas electors."

tions.   The " Union-savers " desired to rouse the nation
to the imminence of the danger before them.   If they failed
in their attempt it would only prove of course, that human
nature was " precisely what it was in the days of Noah." [1]

The leaders of both the sectional parties asserted that the
election of their respective candidates meant no danger to
the Union and both sets of leaders denied the sectional
character of their respective parties.[2]   The Breckinridge
men had some foundation for their claim for there were
northerners who were ready at all times to concede to the
southerners every iota of their constitutional rights ad-
judged them by the Supreme Court of the United States.
This was all the so-called southern extremists asked,
although the Republican opposition repeatedly asserted
that the slave power contemplated aggressions on northern rights, and would be satisfied with nothing less than
making free states into slave states.   There was no state
in the north where Breckinridge did not receive some
votes.   Relatively the number was small but Breckinridge
had over 6,000 supporters in Maine, nearly 2,000 in Ver-
mont, nearly 6,000 in Massachusetts, and over 14,000 in
Connecticut.[3]   Lincoln had absolutely none in ten states of
the Union.   The Republican was the only out-and-out
sectional party when the acid test of geographical membership is applied.   The absolutely negative reaction of ten
(practically fourteen) states to the Republican proposals
and candidate proves conclusively that whatever else the
Republicans might say for themselves they could not truthfully say that their following was national and, therefore,
that their party was a " national" party.

[1] James O. Harrison's unprinted sketches of public men, p. 60.   "Oh!
this general listlessness at such a time was a sad mistake and shows that
the human nature of today is precisely what it was in the days of Noah."

[2] Boston *Atlas* and *Bee*, Aug. 17, 1860, presents a good example of the
attitude of the Republican papers.

[3] Stanwood, *History of the Presidency*, p. 297.

CHAPTER III

THE CAMPAIGN OF 1860

"PARTY PLATFORMS," says a sage, "are made to get off and on by, and not to stand on." In fact it would be a very unusual sight in these days to find a presidential candidate standing with both feet squarely on the party platform in every section of the country. Platforms must contain, of course, some definite statements with but one logical interpretation, obviously meaning but one thing. But some planks of the platform must be so skillfully worded that a variety of interpretations can be logically given to their contents in order that as many voters as possible may be satisfied that the party's platform is in accord with their opinions. For to be serviceable in winning the allegiance of great numbers of voters a platform must be elastic and plastic. Therefore, platforms contain a stock of general statements which nobody will challenge instead of the detailed and specific program which the party leaders intend to follow on the issue touched upon in the general statements. Even the general statements have point to them, the main object of which is to avoid alienating any possible support from the party ticket. The term " rotten plank "[1] has been used to designate the general statement variety—doubtless because it enables the politicians to fool some of the people of the time in regard to the party's bona fide program. Another method of camouflaging the actual policies of party leaders has been termed the "hidden

[1] The term "rotten plank" seems to have meant a plank that a candidate could stand on with only one foot.

plank," which variety is not in the ostensible platform at all. A "hidden plank" conceals a policy on which a number of the party leaders are agreed but which they do not deem wise or necessary to give publicity to as an integral part of the official party program. Thus, the construction of a successful party platform requires a knowledge of the likes and dislikes of the possible party consti- tuents.

The party platforms of 1860 bear the hall-marks of the successful platform. The slavery planks in the Bell platform was of the " hidden variety." The party leaders relied on the party press and orators in the various sections of the country to explain their intentions on this question. However, the Bell platform had a very concrete statement against sectional political parties and the deceitfulness of the platforms of such parties. The Douglas and Breckinridge platforms also had planks expressing condemnation of sectional political parties. The Republican platform said nothing derogatory of sectional parties *per se* but charged the Buchanan administration with wielding the federal government to promote southern sectional interests. However, the Republican platform contained a retort to the charge of sectionalism hurled at it by the other parties. It consisted in an attack upon those who talked of disunion in the event of Republican success. For the southerners to dissolve the Union because they failed to win the election was declared traitorous to the most beneficient form of government in the world, and the Republicans called upon the inhabitants of the northern states to rebuke and silence such traitors by voting the Republican ticket. From a tactical point of view there is much to be said for this method of reply to the charge of sectionalism. " Never defend yourself," says the English maxim, " before a popular assemblage, except with and by retorting the attack: the hearers, in the pleasure which the attack gives them, will forget the previous charge." [1]

All the platforms professed directly or indirectly to be heartily in favor of the Constitution, the Union and the Enforcement of the Law. The territorial slavery question was the cause for this unanimous outburst of legal and patriotic fervor. The Constitution of the United States as the Fathers of American government had made it was the source of inspiration for each party's territorial slavery program. Each maintained that its own particular program was the program which the Fathers would sanction were they still on earth to make their views known and was therefore, in perfect accord with the original method pursued by the Fathers in dealing with the question of slavery in the territories. The Bell party had the best of the argument on this point, but the Republicans,[2] especially, made up in zeal and plausibility of their statements what they lacked in historical and legal fact. "Most assuredly," argued the Americans (as the Constitutional Unionists or Bell party was often called) "under the compromises of the Constitution, the South has just as much right to demand the indiscriminate spread of slavery at the hands of the people, as the North has to demand its arbitrary check. While our fundamental law (the Constitution) exists, the question is settled in favor of neither side (arbitrarily) . . . . Yet this is the precedent which Honest Abe weaves into weary platitudes to demonstrate that the example of our fathers is in favor of modern Republicanism. Abraham should not split the record and sit his lean person on the edge." [3] The extreme southern interpretation of the

[1] Wallas's *Human Nature in Politics*, p. 113.

[2] See Lincoln's Cooper Union speech for Republican views.

[3] *Louisville Journal*, letter of July 1, 1860.

Constitution was that which the Supreme Court of the United States had pronounced authoritative in the dictum accompanying the Dred Scott decision. The Supreme Court is the constitutional arbiter of legal disputes in regard to the meaning of the Constitution. Its decision, though not infallible, is final, until the American people through a constitutional amendment change the Constitution by the affirmative vote of three-fourths of the states. However, a dictum of the Court is not the same as a decision. Strictly speaking, a dictum has not the force of law, but is an anticipatory avowal of what the court will declare the law to be in case the Court has an opportunity to render a decision in a case involving the law declared in the dictum.

The southern platform contained a hidden plank in regard to what some of the southern leaders would undertake to do if the author of the House-Divided speech should be elected president of the whole United States by northern votes, even though the election was entirely in accord with the forms prescribed by law. It had to be a " hidden plank," doubtless, because the States Rights men of the extreme south were not at all sure that they could persuade their constituents to meet the election of a purely sectional candidate with secession. According to the South Carolinian Senator² who spent the summer in the mountains of Virginia ("which region abounded in politicians of every hue and from every part of the country save New England ") most of the States Rights men of the South were well satisfied that their respective states would not meet the election of Lincoln by secession but were likely to await an " overt act " of aggression, though it would then be too late to organize resistance. With one or two exceptions they all urged South Carolina to lead off and take the chances of dragging the others after her; and individually

¹ Hammond papers, Chestnut to Hammond, Oct. 17, 1860.

the southern States Rights men promised to come to her aid and bring their friends. The South Carolinian thought that "the question is too momentous to be left to the urgency and decision of those in other states whose people have decided or will decide not to withdraw." Although Breckinridge, the candidate of the extreme South for the national presidency, was asked repeatedly whether the southern Democrats contemplated withdrawing from the Union in the event of the election of the Black Republican, and although he made a speech at Ashland, the home of Henry Clay, expressly for the purpose of relieving himself and his party of the charge of contemplated disunion, he did not answer the question. He made, however, a powerful presentation of the essential principles of American government, which derived its just powers from the consent of both the North and the South, and he emphasized the function of the Supreme Court under our system. He asserted that there were not over fifty disunionists *per se* in the South and that he was in favor of the Union and the Constitution as the Fathers had drafted it: and declared himself intellectually convinced that no political party had the right to usurp the function of the Supreme Court.

The neutrals preached throughout the South that the election of Lincoln would not be a sufficient cause for secession, and also that the South should vote against the southern sectional candidate and thus hold out an olive branch to the North. They pressed very vigorously the accusation of disunionist intentions on the part of the extreme southern Democrats. The election in the slave states turned largely on the above mentioned campaign arguments of the neutrals. As a result the neutrals had a majority in eight of the slave states, Virginia, Kentucky, Missouri, Maryland, Delaware, Tennessee, Georgia and

Louisiana; and they received over 45 per cent of the vote in three of the others, North Carolina, Arkansas and Alabama.

The neutrals even accused the southern Democrats of engineering a split in the Democratic party for the purpose of making possible the election of Lincoln and thus getting an excuse for secession. This accusation is without adequate foundation; for, if the entire opposition to Lincoln had been united on one candidate, the electoral college would still have given Lincoln the presidency, regardless of the fact that the popular vote against him was a million more than that for him. The system of electing the president made it impossible for the result of this election to register the choice of the American people. More than one American of that day doubtless felt that the manipulation of the constitutional machinery of election by a sectional league such as the Republican party was felt to be, was, " while regular in form, a fraud upon the Constitution and utterly subversive of its spirit." [1]

In the northern free states there were several issues which contained vote-winning qualities beside that of the territorial slavery question. Doubtless one of the points on which the election turned was the conviction that the hidden plank in the southern platform lacked authoritativeness. Breckinridge's Ashland speech was widely quoted as declaring that the southern party was no Disunion party. However, Breckinridge had not said that the South would not consider the election of Lincoln cause for disunion. He maintained that the South was for the " Union and the Constitution " not as a sectional party interpreted it but as the Supreme Court interpreted it. The turning point seems to have been in the North on the fact that the northern people

[1] Bell papers, Washington Hunt to Bell, Nov., 1860.

could not be convinced that the election of Lincoln by a northern sectional party would be considered a just cause for secession by the southern people. The only alternatives in the event of secession were either dissolution of the Union or the rejection by the North of consent as the essential principle of government in so far as the seceding states were concerned. Given secession as a fact, the gist of the matter was then: " Were the northern people willing either to sacrifice the union or to engage in civil war (accepting force as the essential principle of government for the South), for the sake of making a declaration in favor of freedom ·in the territories where freedom was to exist anyway by the law of nature? " Thus, the northern people were called upon to consider not only whether they were in favor of a declaration of freedom in the territories, but also, to decide how badly they wanted to make such a declaration.

The Republican platform contained a " rotten plank " on the main point at issue, namely, what the party would do in case of secession. This plank consisted in a quotation from the Declaration of Independence in regard to the inalienable rights of man, and to a government's deriving its just powers from the consent of the governed. This quotation was incorporated to gain the allegiance of the abolitionists whom Lincoln had held out hopes to in the House-Divided speech and whom Seward had catered to in his " Irrepressible Conflict " oration. It was understood to have reference to including the negroes within the scope of the liberty mentioned among the inalienable rights of man.[1] In addition to the quotation from the Declaration, the plank also contained the following clause: " That the Federal Constitution, the rights of the States and the Union of the States must and shall be preserved." This clause was

[1] Rhodes, vol. ii, pp. 230, 463, 464.

doubtless tacked on for conservative consumption and was calculated to quiet any nervousness caused by the incorporation under such peculiar circumstances of the quotation from the Declaration. However, it is impossible to reconcile the first and last parts of the plank, if both parts were to be carried out as the party's program. If the Republicans embraced the negro under the Declaration, they would have to violate the recognized rights of the southern states. If they preserved the rights of the states intact, they would have to forego their intention to expand the Declaration to embrace the negro. It was thus impossible for the candidate to stand on this plank with more than one foot at a time.

Furthermore, the " rotten " plank's use of the words of Andrew Jackson in regard to the preservation of the union of the States, suggested to the uninformed, and doubtless led them to conclude, that the discontent in the South over the Republican policies of 1860 could not be greater than the discontent at the time when Jackson used the words " must and shall be preserved " in regard to the union of the states when South Carolina nullified the federal tariff law of 1832. It so happened that in 1860, a number of northern states had acts on their statute books, nullifying the federal fugitive slave law. Nullification and secession were both rights of a state according to the States Rights School of statesmen. The references to the preservation of the union and the rights of the States in the Republican platform condoned the nullification of the northern states and at the same time condemned that of the southern states. Evidently the party leaders had a number of purposes in mind when writing this plank, but chief among them was a desire to assist in the election of Lincoln. Nevertheless, the plank lacked precision. It made no definite statement in regard to the most vital point involved in relation to the whole subject with which the plank dealt, namely, what program the Republican administration would pledge to embark upon in case the southern states did secede from the Union upon the election of the northern sectional candidate.

The neutrals made the most strenuous effort to enlighten the northern voters as to the distrust of a northern sectional president which permeated the entire South and to induce the Republican leaders to make some clear-cut acknowledgment of the seriousness of the consequences which might easily result should the southern leaders execute their resolves in the event of the election of a president with irrepressible conflict proclivities. They tried to demonstrate to the northern voter how easily it would be for the southerners to conclude that the election of a president of the above mentioned type by a sectional league, in itself, constituted a partial denial of the full right of self-government to the southern whites. They tried to convince the northern voters that what Burke had said of the American colonies applied with equal force to the people of the southern slave states at this time, namely: "In other countries people more simple and of less mercurial caste, judge of an ill principle by actual experience. Here [in America] they anticipate the evil, and judge of the purpose of the grievance by the badness of the principle. They augur misgovernment at a distance, and snuff tyranny in the tainted breeze."

The Republican leaders sought to convince the northern voter that there would be no just cause for secession in the event of the election of the sectional president: that the southern leaders were only bluffing and were trying to intimidate the northern voter into voting against the dictates of his conscience. Seward, the author of the "Irrepressible Conflict" oration, explained that "the South would never in a moment of resentment expose themselves to war with the North while they have such a great domestic population of slaves ready to embrace any opportunity to assert their freedom and inflict revenge." [1] He further explained that the election of Lincoln would terminate the conflict which he had prophesied—not begin it. [2] "Vote for us," he cried, "and you will have peace and harmony and happiness in your future years." [3] And again he said, "When the Republicans are in office, what may we expect then? . . . I answer, "No dangers, no disasters, no calamities . . . . All parties and sections will alike rejoice in the settlement of the controversy which has agitated the country and disturbed its peace so long." [4] However, the New York Herald openly accused Seward of "pussyfooting." Seward, it asserted, was "a moderate anti-slavery man at Detroit, a radical abolitionist at Lansing, a filibusterer at St. Paul, and the Brother Seward of John Brown did not hesitate to claim to be a good conservative, Union-loving patriot in New York." [5] The election of Lincoln, according to Salmon P. Chase, another of the Republican leaders, would mean a restoration of the old days of concord and good will between the North and the South, "Tranquility, liberty and Union under the Constitution." [6] Greeley, the Republican editor whose paper had the largest circulation of any paper in the United States, solemnly assured his readers that the election of Lincoln would be "like oil on troubled waters and would promptly remove all sectional

---

[1] Black's *Black*, pp. 141-142.

[2] Seward's speech at Chicago, Oct. 3, 1860.

[3] Seward's speech at St. Paul, Sept. 18, 1860.

[4] Seward's speech at Dubuque, Iowa, Sept., 1860.

[5] *New York Herald*, Nov. 1, 1860.

[6] Chase's speech reviewed in *New York Evening Post*, in editorial entitled "What the Republicans will do when they get the power," Aug. 25, 1860.

excitement." And the National Republican Executive Committee closed its last appeal for votes as follows: " We earnestly exhort you to renewed and unceasing efforts until triumph is complete—a triumph which is only desirable because it will bring peace and prosperity to the country and to the world." [1] Carl Schurz, whom the newly arrived Germans followed and whom he usually addressed in their own tongue, explained to one of his audiences that a dissolution of the Union by the South was impossible for several reasons. Among these reasons were the weakness of the South, their divisions among themselves, the danger from their own slaves and their own cowardice. He said that there was no danger of secession. " There had been two overt attempts already—one, the secession of the Southern students from the medical school at Philadelphia, which he ridiculed abundantly; the second, upon the election of Speaker Pennington, when the South seceded from Congress, went out, took a drink, and then came back. The third attempt would be, he prophesied, when Old Abe should be elected. They would then again secede and this time would take two drinks but come back again." It was reported that these sarcasms were received with a roar of deafening shouts by a New England audience.[2]

Matters, other than slavery and secession, came in for a share of the attention in the North. Greater prosperity was desired at that time, especially by the ironmongers of Pennsylvania and other manufacturing districts who wanted a protctive tariff to assist in recouping recent financial reverses. The Democrats refused to incorporate a protective tariff plank in their platform, although it was known that they would have little hope of carrying Pennsylvania

---

[1] Dated Astor House, Oct. 10, 1860, published in *New York Tribune*, Oct. 11, 1860.

[2] Account published in the *Yeoman* (Ky.), Dec. 15, 1860.

without a promise of protection to the iron interests. The Republican platform contained a protective plank and the benefits accruing to certain northern manufacturing districts from the adoption of this policy was sufficient in itself to secure their allegiance to the Republican candidate regardless of the slavery question. After secession had actually taken place and Mr. Lincoln was on his way to Washington for inauguration, he stopped at a few strategic places in Pennsylvania and assured the tariff-loving inhabitants that whatever else Republicanism might mean it meant a beneficent protective tariff.[1] It did not seem to occur to him when he arrived in Pittsburgh that any other matter at that time should take precedence of the tariff.

Plain honesty was also of prime importance as an issue in the presidential campaign of 1860. President Lincoln afterward said that he owed all he was to his reputation for honesty. Senator Grimes of Iowa, felt that the Republican triumph of 1860 was due more to Lincoln's reputed honesty and the known corruption of the Democratic administration at Washington than because of the territorial slavery question. He wrote as follows to Senator Trumbull of Illinois, just after the result of the election became known: "We have in our party as corrupt a set of d—ls as there is in the world—known of all men to be so, who will be the fiercest to secure places of responsibility and value. Now our triumph was achieved more because of Lincoln's reputed honesty and the known corruption of the Democrats than because of the negro question. Our President I hope will remember this."[2] There is ample reason to believe that

[1] Speech at Pittsburgh, Pa., Feb. 15, 1861. The opening sentence of the speech contains the gist of the remarks: " Fellow citizens, as this is the first opportunity I have had to address a Pennsylvania assembly it seems a fitting time to indulge in a few remarks on the important question of the tariff."

[2] Trumbull papers, Nov. 13, 1860.

Senator Grimes was not exaggerating the importance of the honesty of Honest Abe as one of the deciding factors in the presidential contest of 1860.[1] The Covode Committee appointed by Congress to investigate the Buchanan administration's conduct of public affairs had presented a damaging report in plenty of time to be thoroughly circulated all over the North. The *New York Tribune* published the report of what would now be called the Republican " Smelling Committeee " and stated that " so startling an exposition of corruption in high places was never before submitted to the American people." [2] The report was extremely partisan in its nature but with enough truth to make it extremely effective campaign material for the Republicans. The obvious conclusion was that a change of party was imperatively needed at Washington. The Republican papers during the entire campaign and the Constitutional Unionist papers up to the time of their fusion with the Douglas Democrats, gave a great deal of attention to the lack of integrity of the Democrats.

[1] See Chase papers, Nash to Chase, April 9, 1860. " Now there were certain things honest men were tired of, disgusted with. One of these was a mere partisan administration. Partisanship has corrupted all the avenues of office and all comers of the government, so much so that a Democrat said to me, an honest account could not be passed at Washington unless paid for. . . . Men hoped for better things, had rejected Democracy for this reason, *etc.*"

See also Crittenden papers, Reed to Crittenden, Jan. 17, 1861. " Multitudes voted the Republican ticket because we wanted honesty to displace corruption. We do not hesitate to say we prefer the non-extension of slavery but we are not so immovably tenacious of this principle as to insist upon it literally in the face of civil war." And also a letter of Jan. 16, Spoford to Crittenden.

See also Lamon's *Lincoln*, p. 460. Lincoln said: " All that I am in the world—the Presidency and all else—I owe to that opinion of me which the people express when they call me ' Honest Old Abe.' Now what will they think of their honest Abe when he appoints Simon Cameron to be his familiar advisor."

[2] *New York Tribune*, June, 1860.

The partial fusion of the nationalistic neutrals took place toward the middle of the summer when it became understood that the secession movement was really scheduled to take place in the event of Lincoln's election. The only hope of the fusionists seems to have been to throw the election into the House of Representativies by preventing Lincoln from gaining a majority of the electoral votes. In case they could accomplish this it was calculated that John Bell, the Unionist nominee, would be most likely to be the successful candidate.[1] The political complexion of the Senate guaranteed the choice of Joseph Lane, the running mate of John C. Breckinridge, as vice-president. If the House failed to make a choice for president then Lane would succeed to the presidency. Unfortunately for the cause of fusion in the North, Lane was the choice of the Buchanan administration and this administraion was unpopular throughout the North not only on account of the revelations of the Covode Committee but also on account of its record in attempting to bring in Kansas as a slave state when the Kansas had voted a free-state Constitution. Herein lay the greatest weakness of the fusion movement because the northern voter keenly felt that Lane was as sectional a candidate as Lincoln—they could not see the point in renouncing the northern sectional candidate by voting the fusion ticket and thereby bringing about the election of Lane in the Senate.

The Republicans contrived to associate the idea of corruption with the fusion movement also. After a fusion ticket had been adopted in New York, Greeley filled the

[1] Apparently, if the election went to the House of Representatives, Bell had the best chance of election. He was the least objectionable of the opponents to the partisan followers of the other three. For the same reason that Pennington won the speakership in 1859, Bell would have been likely to have won the presidency in 1860, had the election been thrown into the House.

columns of the *Tribune* with " righteous indignation " at
the " fraud." The frustration of the fusion movement was
vital to the success of the Republican candidate. The
Tribune bristled with such phrases as " humbug," " shallow
and transparent humbug," "·enormous humbug," " nasty
intrigue," " swindle," " cheat," " corrupt bargain and
sale " with reference to the fusion of the nationalistic
neutrals. " The mellow voices· of the Know-Nothings are
to mingle with the rich Irish brogue and sweet German ac-
cent around the wooden pillars of Tammany Hall," the
Greeley paper announced and proceeded to denounce the
leaders of the movement as " truckling politicians and
knavish schemers," and as " shallow and tricky dema-
gogues." " The fusion," the paper asserted, " was one of
politicians and not of the people " and " the mistake of the
wireworkers inheres in their forgetting that the People are
honest and earnest." Bragging and lying, according to
Greeley, were the chief weapons of the coalition. A million dollars had been raised to buy up the people of New
York but the Tribune held that it was " the inalienable
right of white men not to be sold without their consent."
    The purpose of the coalition was to sell the Bell men to
Douglas, this astute paper discovered, and then deliver
them bound hand and foot to Gen. Joe Lane. For, the purpose of the coalition was manifestly to defeat the will of the
People by throwing the election into Congress. This
would undoubtedly result in the election of Joe Lane in the
Senate, declared the great Republican editor, and the Republican press all over the North made it appear very vividly
and emphatically that the fusionists were being made a cat's
paw for Joe Lane'e chestnuts. And it demonstrated again
and again that Lincoln was the only candidate who had
a chance of receiving a majority vote in the electoral college which the Republican press treated as a synonym for

"the People." It also showed that the only chance of the opposition was to throw the election into Congress, which the Republicans felt would produce a "carnival of faction" and a "deep and injurious agitation of the whole country" and finally would result in the election of Joe Lane by the Senate, who would "perpetuate and intensify the evils experienced under the administration of Mr. Buchanan." Thus, Greeley and the other Republican editors proved that there was no middle ground possible between Lincoln and Lane, an honest Republican and a corrupt Democrat. They made it appear that it was necessary to swallow Lincoln to avoid Lane.[1] Nor did they neglect to point out that the coalition was trying to cheat the Irish and the Germans who would not knowingly vote for a Know-Nothing, while at the same time the coalition was trying to make believe that "the Douglas men would go snacks with the debris of the defunct Know-Nothing organization."

In spite of the chorus from the Republican press, the nationalistic neutrals continued to call upon the average American voter to steer the ship of state between the Scylla and Charybdis of northern and southern sectionalism. The neutrals won a majority in eleven states. Only three of these were free states, but the fact that they received over 49 per cent of the vote in Illinois, over 48 per cent of the vote in Indiana, over 47 per cent in Pennsylvania and Ohio, over 46 per cent in New York and over 45 per cent in Iowa, indicates that there was no such thing as a solid North on the territorial slavery policy advocated by the Republican party. The heavy nationalistic neutral vote in the South

---

[1] The Lincoln or Lane point was tremendously stressed, as the files of the Republican newspapers amply testify. See Boston *Daily Advertiser*, Nov. 1, 2, 3, and Oct. 31; New York *Evening Post*, Aug. 28, Sept. 29; *New York Tribune*, Aug. 1, July 25, 30, 23, Sept. 20, 27, Oct. 4; *Cincinnati Commercial*, July 28, Oct. 6, 24; *Worcester Spy*, Oct. 3 and 10; *Hartford Courant*, Aug. 20, etc.

indicated that the solid South was certainly not bent on spreading slavery into the territories—much less into the free states. It indicated even, that the South preferred the Union without slavery eventually to slavery without the Union, for neither Douglas nor Bell held out any hope for another slave state. In the face of this vote it is folly to assert that the southern people were aggressively pro-slavery and bent on maintaining slavery at any cost. It is also impossible to conclude, when one takes into consideration the arguments and statements stressed by the Republican orator and press during the campaign, that the Republican administration received instructions to so conduct itself before and on entering office that a war on behalf of the negro would inevitably result.

Very few southerners took northern newspapers and very few northerners took southern newspapers and so it happened that a really dangerous situation existed. George D. Prentice of the *Louisville Journal* wrote Lincoln on October 26, requesting him in the event of the success of the Republicans in the electoral colleges to write a letter setting forth conservative views and intentions. Prentice promised to publish such a letter in the Journal, the paper which had the largest circulation of any one paper in the slave states. Prentice's purpose was to check the agitation which he felt so certain to break out in the South as soon as the victory of the Black Republican became positively ascertained. Lincoln made a very astute reply to Prentice, referring Prentice to the already published speeches for his " conservative views and intentions." [1]   Unfortunately the average southerner felt that if the published speeches of Lincoln were to be taken before any jury, the jury would feel compelled to convict Lincoln of believing in negro emancipation and negro equality.

[1] Nicolay and Hay, *Complete Works of Abraham Lincoln*, vol. ii, pp. 66-67.

CHAPTER IV

Government of, by and for the People

After reading volumes of judgments on the wrong of secession, now, when the smoke of battle has somewhat cleared away, and after reviewing the evidence from which these judgments were drawn, one is gradually forced to conclude that the secessionists have been denied justice at the bar of history on one point at least. The great historian of the period withholds absolution from the southerners when he declares that secession was a precipitate movement to break the bonds of union with states whose offence lay in the declaration that slavery was wrong and should not be extended.[1] Doubtless at the time secession was taking place many northern conservatives who voted for Lincoln felt that such was an accurate and complete account of the secession movement. But acceptance for the absolute truth of so simple an estimate as that which was native to the northern conservatives who voted for Lincoln, is, politically speaking, a trifle naïve. Inasmuch as the majority of southern people had voted for Douglas and Bell in the presidential election and thereby signified that they did not care whether slavery was or was not extended, or what the Republicans thought and declared about slavery, so long as they did not interfere with the labor system and civilization of the South, the historian's explanation cannot apply to the majority of southerners. And

[1] Rhodes, vol. iii, p. 117.

obviously no statement which does not include a consideration of the majority is an accurate account.   As to secession
being precipitate, secession had been deliberated upon for
years,[1] Senator Hammond of South Carolina, had taught
that union with the northern states was a "policy" and not
a "principle."[2]   It is perfectly true that the northern people
were unprepared for the secession of South Carolina—
much less, for that of the other southern states; for they
had been solemnly assured by their trusted leaders that the
South was bluffing.   Therefore secession seemed precipitate to them; but as a matter of fact the discussion pre-
ceding South Carolina's action was of such length as to
give it the character of mature deliberation.   Actual secession and the organization of the southern confederacy
could hardly have been executed by hot-headed school boys
on the spur of the moment as the word "precipitate" im-
plies.   Under the circumstances secession may have been
unwise but it can hardly be termed precipitate.

It is apparent that the people of South Carolina were the
only people of any of the southern states who thought that
the election of Lincoln was sufficient cause in itself for
breaking the bonds of the Union.   South Carolina was the
home state of what may be termed the secessionists *per se.*
This group, comparatively small in number as compared
with the whole southern people, had come to believe that it
was to the permanent interest of the Gulf States at least, if
not of all the slave states, to be under a separate government
from the northern states.   General incompatibility, arising
from a difference in geographical location, with its attendant
difference in commercial interests, and from a difference in
opinion in regard to the appropriate condition of the

[1] That is to say, secession in South Carolina.

[2] Hammond papers, Hammond to Simms, July 10, 1860.

negroes, was the underlying basis for the South Carolinians' desire for divorce from the manufacturing states and especially from the state of Massachusetts, the home of Charles Sumner. The following resolutions suggested by Senator Hammond give the inflammatory argument of the South Carolinan secessionists who promptly seceded from the Union when the news came that a Black Republican had been constitutionally elected president of the United States of America:

Recent events having placed the Chief Power of the Federal Government in the hands of a Party, Organization, League, perhaps most accurately to be denominated a conspiracy which is purely sectional and entirely confined to the non-slaveholding states of this Union, and which has beforehand through all its leading organs declared that between said states and the slaveholding states there is an " irrepressible conflict," which has proclaimed that its purpose is to exercise all the power of the government to the restriction and extinction of African slavery in the United States and territories: which has already before getting into power, instigated war and has actually carried it on with arms and bloodshed, with incendiary torches and poison, all brought to bear fatally and extensively upon a peaceable and unoffending people reposing for the most part with entire good faith upon the guarantees of a common constitution and the pledges of a most intimate alliance; which scoffs at our complaints of these unjust and unconstitutional assaults upon our rights and interests and inhuman and fiendlike war upon our households and hearthstones, on our wives and daughters and ourselves, etc.[1]

As has been stated the South Carolinians were the only people who were thoroughly convinced that the time had arrived for a dissolution of the Union. Nevertheless, the secession of South Carolina took place with the advice and consent of leaders from other states, both slave and free.

Undoubtedly these leaders knew that the whole north was

[1] Hammond papers, Hammond to Hayne, Sept. 19, 1860.

not abolitionized; but undoubtedly the irrepressible conflict proclivities of the President-elect and the " rotten " plank in the Chicago platform gave them great uneasiness for the future.   In treating of secession historians have the habit of eliding the significance of the " rotten " plank in the Chicago platform.   But it cannot be assumed that the southern leaders were not aware of the full possibilities of that plank. They had no guarantee that the policy of the President-elect who had annexed an abolitionist wing for flight into office would not be controlled by the radical wing of the party. They had no confidence in Lincoln's good intentions toward the southern people for they had reached the conclusion that any intelligent person who asserted, as Lincoln had asserted,[1] that Jefferson had the negroes in mind when he wrote the Declaration of Independence, belonged in the class of mischievous agitators, so obvious was it to them that Jefferson fully recognized the existence of African slavery.   The John Brown raid was fresh in the memory of the southern people and needless to say the southern people were hardly in a position to look upon the " rotten " plank in the Chicago platform with the same complacency and simple faith which the northern conservative exercised while interpreting it.[2]

However, the public opinion of the world today ap-

[1] Rhodes, vol. ii, p. 230.

[2] See address of John C. Breckinridge before the Kentucky Legislature, Dec. 21, 1859. " The danger springs from the character and purposes of a political organization in this country called the Republican party, what it intends, and the probable consequences of its success in the United States. . . . At first it seemed to limit its aims to the exclusion of slavery from the Territories; but, like all aggressive organizations, its course has been continually onward. The rear rank of the Republican army marches up and encamps on the ground occupied by the advanced guards months before, while the advanced guard has been marching steadily forward." A pamphlet in the James O. Harrison papers contains this address.

parently justifies the Civil War because the Declaration of Independence portion of the "rotten" plank of the Chicago platform was summarily incorporated as a *bona fide* part of the Republican party's program. The notion that one cannot do right in the wrong way is now applauded in connection with the consummation of liberation at the point of the sword, a process which was very nearly the equivalent of a huge John Brown raid into the southern states. The public of today has apparently reached the conclusion that the civilization which produced Washington, Jefferson, Patrick Henry, Madison, Clay, John Marshall and Robert E. Lee, was too unutterably brutal to be permitted to adjust itself to modern conditions and deserved to perish by the sword. It is hard for the public of today to realize that the public of 1860-1861 had an entirely different opinion. It did not occur to the mass of northern people of that day that the precipitate abolition of slavery in the southern states would be profitable even to the negroes themselves.

There is no evidence to show that the American people of that day, not only the Americans who lived in the slave states, but also the vast majority of Americans who lived in the free states, thought the negro capable of skipping over the tendencies which the white man had derived from thousands of years of his self-developed civilization, and passing with a few years training or without a few years training, from the mental condition and inheritance of barbarians and slaves into full equality with the free citizens of a self-governing republic, whose laws, traditions, habits and customs, were totally alien, far more alien than those of the Japanese and Chinese. The Americans of that day did not feel that a mere statute law permitting the negro to equal the white man in autonomous government could enable him to do so. The slave system was regarded fundamentally not as a matter of morals, of right and wrong, but merely as an economic arrangement which was essentially the outgrowth of an inequality and difference in inheritance between the average white and black man. It is safe to say that all of the southerners and most of the northerners knew that the negroes were not a race resembling angels in ability to pass from one extreme to the other without passing through the middle.

Therefore, it cannot be said that there was basic antagonism between the northern and the southern people in regard to the slavery question in the southern states. The objections of the northerners to the slave system were not to the slave system itself but to the by-products of the system. These by-products were the so-called southern aristocrat and the necessity for northerners to return fugitive slaves. These two items constitute the sum total of the real differences between the North and the South in so far as the negro was concerned. There can be no doubt that among the newly arrived immigrants and among persons belonging to the class from which Lincoln arose there was a special feeling that the southern aristocrats felt that there were but two kinds of people in the world, themselves and common people. The negroes seem to have felt that there were three kinds of people, ranking as follows : southern aristocrats, negroes and common people. However, if one is to judge the existence of a democracy by a feeling of equality among the people of a nation there is no such thing as democracy on earth. As to the other objectionable by-product, the return of fugitives, it is clear that this was extremely annoying to some of the good northern people, especially to New Englanders, who were coming to think of slavery in terms of Uncle Tom's Cabin and not in terms of the then unwritten stories of Thomas Nelson Page or of the sentiment depicted in " Way Down on the Suwanee

River." However, the existence of these two " feelings "
among certain northerners did not prevent them from being
in sympathy with the southern people on the essentials
which constitute a nation, for, they practiced the same form
of government, obeyed the same laws (including the fugitive
slave law), they took pride in a common history, they wor-
shipped at the same altar, they used the same language, they
read the same books (except a very few), they carried on
an extensive and lucrative commerce with each other; in a
word, there were more ties to bind than there were barriers
to separate the people of the North and the South.

If there was any really vital difference between the
North and the South, it was on what constituted a
sectional control of the national government. Many
who voted for Lincoln did not consider him any more
sectional than Breckinridge or Lane, whom the extremists
of the South championed. They felt that if the South
thought it proper to have Breckinridge as president, they
could not see why it was not equally proper for them to
have Lincoln, especially, when they had constitutionally
elected him.[1] However, a majority of the southern people
did not vote for Breckinridge, but registered themselves in
favor of the two national candidates. The Republican
leaders did not admit that theirs was a sectional party.
Their usual reply to the charge of sectionalism was " Slavery is sectional, freedom is national." This line of argument seems to have completely muddled the minds of many
honest northerners on the difference between a " national "
and a " sectional " party and control of the government.
They failed to realize that the Republican party of 1860

[1] Hammond papers, A. B. Allen to Hammond, N. Y., Jan. 22, 1861 :
" Ninety-nine out of every hundred of my party deny in the most emphatic manner that we have elected a sectional candidate. He is not
half as much sectional as Breckinridge."

answered perfectly to Washington's definition of a geographical party against the formation of which he solemnly warned his fellow-countrymen in the Farewell Address.   In view of the " Lincoln or Lane " cry of the Republican politicians during the presidential campaign, in view of the desire of the mass of the northern people for an honest administration of the national government such as they felt " Honest Abe " (judging him by his nickname) would give, in view of the assurance given them by their trusted leaders and the only newspapers the majority of them read that the election of Lincoln would peacefully settle the sectional controversy, one cannot conclude that the North was sectionalized.   It seems that if the question of sectionalism had been fairly put and frankly met by the Republican leaders, it is more than likely that the northern people would have given as just a decision as the southern people on the issue of " sectionalism " versus " nationalism."

In view of the basic lack of antagonism between the southern and the northern people, it is hardly reasonable to suppose that a majorty of the southern leaders and southern people desired a permanent dissolution of the union, much less a war with the numerically superior North.   Both of these solutions were *derniers ressorts*.   However, the southern people were not willing to submit quietly to a control of the national government by a northern sectional league whose sense of justice (judged by the statements of the extremists whom the South was prone to regard as typical of the North) seemed abnormally well developed toward the negro but subnormally developed toward the southern white.   Sentiment was very general throughout the South against living under a government controlled by a northern sectional league.   To the southern white man, a government of, by and for the people most emphatically was not a government based solely on northern consent.

The able and vigorous campaign of the nationalists had apparently succeeded in convincing the majority of the southern people that the election of Lincoln would not be a sufficient cause in itself to render necessary such a conclusion. But it seemed wise to a number of southern leaders to nip in the bud the first attempt at sectional control of the national government. And accordingly the secession of South Carolina under the advice of other than South Carolinian leaders cannot be regarded as an attempt to break up the union on account of the election of Lincoln.[1] It was really an attempt to break up the Republican party and a continued control of the national government by a sectional league.[2] The secession of the one state was at first merely an emphatic protest in so far as it can be said to have represented southern sentiment.

After leading off with the secession of one state the southerners followed this secession with the presentation of an ultimatum. This ultimatum was embodied in the Crittenden Compromise, presented to the United States Senate by Senator John J. Crittenden of Kentucky, one of the southern nationalists. The main article of the Crittenden Compromise was the restoration of the line 36° 30′ demolished by Douglas in the Kansas-Nebraska measure as the dividing line between slave and free territory. The southern party relinquished their claim to

[1] Hammond papers, Aldrich to Hammond, Dec. 6, 1860: "Mason, Davis, Brown, Pugh, McQueen and several others, whose names I do not now recollect, all recommend the most prompt action; they say take the State out at once, any delay is dangerous and may be fatal." See also Breckenridge's speech before the Kentucky Legislature. "The first duty of all those who love their country is to overthrow the Republican party."

[2] See "The Stratagem of the Present Excitement" in the *Boston Atlas and Bee*, Dec. 7, 1860, for a northern view of this significance of secession, and Breckinridge papers, John C. B. to R. J. B., Jan. 30, 1860, for a southern view.

federal protection of slavery in all of the national territories, if the northern party would relinquish their demand for prohibition of slavery in all of the territories, and the status quo before the repeal of the Missouri Compromise would be re-established.   The effect of the Crittenden Compromise was of no importance in regard to the actual existence of slavery in the national territories where soil and climate effectively prohibited its profitable use.   Its importance was due to the fact that its acceptance by the Republican leaders in behalf of the Republican party would have annihilated the Republican party.   For, as a result of the settlement of the political controversy over slavery in the territories, the radical and conservative wings of the Republican party would have separated into its original discordant elements, and those whom the political sagacity of Abraham Lincoln had joined together would have been torn asunder.   The southern leaders hoped to force the Republican leaders to clear up the ambiguity of the " rotten " plank on which they stood with only one foot.   The southerners calculated that, thereby, they could limit the anti-slavery tenets of the Republican party to the conservative northern ideal.   It was felt that the conservative wing of the party and in fact, the great majority of the northern people would prefer the Crittenden Compromise to either disunion or civil war.[1]   The acceptance or rejection of the Crittenden Compromise was to be taken as a fair test of the intentions of the Republican leaders, both on the slavery question and on the sectional control of the national government.

---

[1] Hammond papers, Mallory to Hammond, Dec. 27, 1860: " Every northern man I meet who is not a *leader* of Republicanism admits the justice of our complaints and the readiness of the northern people to provide a remedy. . . . If we can stave off bloodshed we shall have a triumphal and peaceful conclusion to our difficulty."   Mallory was one of the United States Senators from Florida.

The Crittenden Compromise was rejected by the Republican party leaders. The test was fairly put and the decision was against the South and in favor of a sectional control of the national government.[1] As a result of this exhibition of intention to continue indefinitely to dictate the policy of the national government on the part of what was felt in the South to be a northern sectional league, six more southern states followed South Carolina out of the Union and the seven proceeded to organize a southern confederacy before the inauguration of the northern sectional candidate. With the rejection of the Crittenden Compromise, an anticipated fact apparently became an established fact in the minds of large numbers of persons who were not disunionists per se. The truth of the matter then in regard to the secession of the six states which immediately followed South Carolina seems to be that the rejection of the Crittenden Compromise convinced them (in the words of Senator Hammond) that "a party, organization, league, or conspiracy" had been formed to control permanently the national government. Disunion and civil war were *derniers ressorts* to these southerners but they preferred both to submitting quietly to what they considered an abrogation of their rights. Although the rejection of the Crittenden Compromise gave an enormous impetus to "secessionism" the people of the eight other slave states remained unconvinced. These remaining unseceded southern people comprised a majority of the southern people. They signified their intention to remain in the Union until some overt act of the administration which had been chosen solely by northern votes should prove beyond all doubt that the radical wing was to dominate its policy. The eight un-

[1] See Toombs' message to the people of Georgia: "The test has been put fairly and frankly, and it is decisive against the South." This was published in the southern press; see Kentucky *Yeoman*, Dec. 27, 1860.

seceded states were, of course, the border slave states, where northern sentiment was much better understood, and whose permanent interests lay in and not out of the Union of all of the states.

Mr. James Ford Rhodes has proved [1] that Lincoln was responsible for the rejection of the Crittenden Compromise, but the Republican leaders and politicians in general opposed its acceptance because it would "lay the Republican party on the shelf." [2]   The disunion of the states was not

[1] Rhodes, vol. iii, pp. 158-166.

[2] The disastrous effect of the Crittenden Compromise on the fortunes of the Republican party was a matter of common knowledge among the party politicians and party workers. See among the Washburne papers the following expressions: "A compromise which should back down on vital principles, would lay us out colder than a wedge" from Judson, Jan. 17, 1861; "If the Republican cause should come down to a compromise they never could get half in this state again" from Baldwin, Jan. 25, 1861; "We must stand firm as a party in maintaining and defending the principles we have contended for the past six years or we are 'gone up'—of this there can be no difference of opinion" from a worker who wanted an appointment to some foreign office where "the duties of office are neither arduous nor complicated" Dec. 20, 1860; "Any other course (than standing firm) will demoralize the party and scatter to the winds the fruition hoped for and to be expected from our great victory" from Sanford, Dec. 4, 1860; "Having conclusive proof that you are strong on your 'pins' and free from any spinal affection, I entreat you with all earnestness to exhort, rebuke, and encourage the faltering, if there are any among the Republicans in Congress, make them to understand that retreat is death, to advance is safety" from Nat Vose, Dec. 15, 1860; "The Republican pulse beats high for war but a backdown to Traitors and Slavery will ruin our party and prospects" from Armstrong, Feb. 12, 1860; "To yield one new guarantee to slavery will either destroy the Republican party or send to their political graves every Republican who lends his support or countenances such a course" from Armour, Dec. 21, 1860; "Any further concessions on the part of the Republicans will be as fatal to them as a snake bite" from Stephenson, Jan. 15, 1861; "They say, and not without cause, that if the Republicans back down to the slave power now that the party shall go to smash, as you no doubt are well aware" from Stewart, Feb. 8, 1861. And also see among the

so important to Salmon P. Chase as the disunion of the Re-

Trumbull papers: "My opinion is that the man or Party that yields to the Slave Power now will soon be consigned to political graves from which there will be no resurrection," from Henderson, Feb. 5, 1861; "Under these circumstances you can easily see that it is the veriest suicide for the party leaders to yield to the demands of the fire-eaters, for it can only result in their being thrown overboard without mercy, etc., of rending the party into a hundred wavering fragments, and by so doing reinstate in power the slavocracy," from Glaucy, Feb. 11, 1860; "We cannot believe that the Republicans in Congress are ready to make political martyrs not only of themselves but of their friends at home, and, in a word, the whole party," and "We fully believe that the whole thing was concocted purposely to bring about the destruction of the Republican party by creating strife and division among them as a party," from Gainco and Crow who believed that they expressed the sentiments of the entire party in their vicinity, Feb. 22, 1861; "If our members of Congress give up one principle which the Republican Party stand upon, we are gone, hook and line," from Woods, Dec. 20, 1860; "I repeat, do not sacrifice the party. If we suffer the principles of the party to be compromised away, the party is dead. We won the victory, it is ours," from Ramer, Feb. 7, 1860; "To let down the Republican platform or essentially abate from its freedom character would be the annihilation of the party," from Talcott, Dec. 16, 1860; "Kept together by no great principle, we as a party would have suffered disintegration. We would have resolved into original and repulsive elements, and the leaders who would have brought that disgrace upon us would have suffered a political death from which no Archangel's trump would have ever awakened them," from Jewett, March 6, 1860; "To compromise is to ruin the Republican Party, for it is to rend it asunder. . . . Let the leaders stand firm. . . . The party will remain a harmonious, triumphant band, ready for conflict, expectant of a long career of unbroken triumph. . . . The vital question for the Republican party is, 'Will Abraham Lincoln stand firm in this trying hour?' We answer, 'He will!'" *New York Tribune*, Feb. 8, 1861. "People have never been able to believe that the secessionists were in downright earnest in their avowed purpose to make a new nation by cutting a few blocks out of the American Union. . . . The unconditional surrender of the Republican party is required," from *Boston Atlas and Bee*, March 27, 1861.

The greatest problem which the Republican leaders were trying to solve at this period was, "Cannot the Republican party preserve the Union and at the same time preserve itself?" The Republican leaders had to choose between saving the party through Civil War and saving

publican party.[1] Chase felt that if the party leaders would stand firm and not yield an inch to conciliate the southerners that the party stood a good chance of controlling the federal government for the next third of the century.   If

the Union by acknowledging that they were wrong in the premises, not wrong on the slavery issue, but wrong in their advocacy of sectional control of the national government. If the party "took up the trade" of peacefully saving the Union like the professional "Union-Savers" of the old Whig school, "it may as well go to the wall" mourned George Hoadly of Cincinnati to Salmon P. Chase. And the "truth" manifestly was, as one of the politicians wrote Washburne, that the whole trouble was to a great extent political, "an intention on the part of the Democrats to force, through fear of Civil War, the Republicans to concede so much as to practically disband the party." Said he, "I would see the devil have the whole South before I would vote for any such measure as the Crittenden Compromise."

The great stumbling-block in the path of the southern statesmen obtaining concessions from the North was that the legislatures of the northern states were in the hands of persons whose political life depended on their not conceding "an inch" to their adversaries. This situation is very clearly shown in a letter to Chase from N. B. Judd of Illinois, Jan. 11, 1861: "There is a severe outside pressure here for some (conciliatory) action by the Republicans in the legislature. Some of our men are alarmed at the aspect of public affairs and desire to do something but do not know what they want and we have trouble in holding them steady. I send you some resolutions upon which I wish your opinion as to their effect upon the position and integrity of the party—and also their propriety as propositions without reference to the condition of the party at present. . . . The Democracy are in state convention today and intend to make concession an issue, with such a population as we have had our small majority, there is danger for us ahead." The same condition is seen in the letter of E. Peck from Illinois to Senator Trumbull, Feb. 2, 1861: "The proposition to send commissioners to Washington (to the Peace Conference called by Virginia) was passed through the General Assembly yesterday, this was done as a matter of political necessity because if we had not united to do so, some of our knock-kneed brethren would have united with the Democracy and would have given them sufficient strength to have the resolutions appointing by the General Assembly." The resolutions gave the appointment of the commissioners to the Republican Governor, and of course they were not "knock-kneed brethren."

[1] Trumbull papers, Trumbull from Chase, Nov. 11, 1860.

they compromised they felt that Lincoln would be the first and last of the Republican presidents. To the average Republican party politician the Crittenden Compromise and the secession of South Carolina, were but a scheme whereby the Republicans would be shortly ousted from office. Doubtless the party worker, who had gotten out the whole vote in his district and had all the unnaturalized Germans to take out papers in time to vote, felt that he deserved a federal postmastership for life.[1] Indeed, there were some workers who had worked in the free soil and liberty party movement for twenty years and these did not feel it incumbent upon them to modestly renounce the results of victory so soon. One after another sent in application or applied in person for federal office. The number of persons who felt that their services deserved the reward of a cabinet position[2] or a foreign post was considerably greater than the number of positions to be filled. The politicians were unanimously in favor of doing nothing which would surrender one iota of political advantage to the party. However, the politicians and office-seekers did not represent the rank and file of the party.

The great mass of conservative voters in the Republican party, represented by Charles Francis Adams of Massachusetts, Thurlow Weed of New York, and Thomas Cor-

---

[1] "We made use of every available piece of timber, had what Republican Germans there were naturalized, who had not previously become citizens and got out *all* the votes." Washburne papers, Nov. 17, 1860. The author of the above quotation was rewarded with a postmastership.

[2] The greatest difficulty was experienced in getting the cabinet positions distributed to the best advantage. Cameron of Pennsylvania had to be included although he was *persona non grata* to the "holier" men of the party. "Can I get along," asked Lincoln, "if that state should oppose my administration?" Koerner's *Memoirs*, vol. ii, p. 114. Gideon Welles of Connecticut was made Secretary of the Navy for similar reasons, although Seward said that Welles did not know the stem of a boat from its stern. Oberholtzer's *Lincoln*, p. 188.

win of Ohio, besides a considerable number of others, were favorable to compromise. They favored some compromise, preferably one offered by a Republican, but they were ready and willing to renounce the essentially sectional character of their party for the sake of a peaceful preservation of the Union. Many a Republican understood that the trend of the times was against the South and that sooner or later the labor system of the South, for purely economic reasons, would have to succumb. These Republicans were even willing to be magnanimous and give the southerners more than the average northerner had been taught to believe that the South could justly claim.[1]   It was with great difficulty

---

[1] William T. Sherman thought that a " declaration of *no more* slave states in advance is offensive and mischievous besides being unnecessary—time enough when one applies for admission. ' Irrepressible conflict' should be a Sewardism, not a party thought. To govern all the country, your Doctrines must be consistent with the interests of all parts of the country." Sherman papers, Oct. 3, 1860. The following also shows the conservative trend of reasoning: " There were thousands and thousands of Conservative men in the North who voted for Lincoln, who would now yield much for the sake of peace and feel that they were not compromising principle thereby. . . . Every year the North is gaining whilst the South loses political power. Lord Wellington said that anything is better than Civil War. . . . He made concessions which his friends insisted were at variance with consistency." Trumbull papers, Trumbull from W. S. Gilman, Dec. 11, 1860. Also see Trumbull from Detrich, March 2, 1861; Trumbull from Lansing, Feb. 17, 1861; Trumbull from Isaac Lea, Dec. 26, 1860; Trumbull from J. M. Richard, Chicago, Jan. 18, 1861. See also Breckinridge papers: McDaniel to R. J. Breckinridge, Jan. 21, 1861, " Majority of Republicans, not radical. . . . Three-fourths in favor of any fair arrangement"; R. L. Allen to R. J. Breckinridge, Jan. 21, 1861, " Northern sentiment modified and has never been a fourth as bad as represented." . . . Also states that " the majority of those who voted for Mr. Lincoln did so with no other views than to secure an upright, conservative administration of our constitution and laws"; that " three-fourths at least, perhaps nine-tenths of the northern voters are ready to sanction any reasonable concession"; and that " among the vast majority of the northern people the same fraternal feeling for their southern

that the radical leaders prevented William H. Seward from offering some adequate compromise to halt the procession of southern states out of the union.[1]   But after Seward accepted the offer of the office of Secretary of State under the incoming administration, he submitted to the leadership of Lincoln.

As Lincoln clearly stated in 1863 there were but three conceivable courses for the Republicans to follow.[2]   Either some compromise had to be made, or the seceding states had to be allowed to go in peace, or the secession movement had to be crushed by force of arms.   With the exception of a small group of secessionists *per se,* the three-fifths of the American people who had voted against Lincoln were undoubtedly in favor of compromise.   Furthermore, since a great number of those voting for Lincoln were also in favor of compromise, it can be truthfully said that an overwhelming majority of both the northern and the southern people preferred compromise to either a dissolution of the Union or Civil War.[3]   The majority of the northern people were perfectly willing to meet the southern people halfway.

brethren exists which has always existed." The great thing to be accomplished according to this R. L. Allen, who had voted for Lincoln, was "to disabuse the South of their false opinion": D. B. Duffield to R. J. Breckinridge, Feb. 17, 1861; S. Holmes to R. J. Breckinridge, Feb. 22, 1861, "I hesitate not to say the great trouble is occasioned by the dust thrown in the eyes of the masses by wild politicians"; L. F. Allen to R. J. Breckinridge, Jan. 10, 1861.

[1] "The unconciliatory and defiant course of the Republican leaders has rendered the advocates of patience and steadiness in the South all but powerless. Beyond dispute, it is the principal cause of the fearful distrust of the North which now possesses and inflames the Southern breast." *Louisville Journal,* Dec. 31, 1860.

[2] Lincoln to Conkling, Aug. 26, 1863, published in one of the Illinois State Historical Society publications.

[3] Northern historians from Greeley to Rhodes acknowledge this to be a fact.

The election returns had shown that the southern people were not bent on nationalizing slavery as the political agitators had asserted for they had voted for Douglas and Bell, leaders who did not promise the extension of slavery into any of the territories.   The pressure for the adoption of the Crittenden Compromise was enormous, especially when it became known that Davis and Toombs were willing to accept it as a final settlement of the territorial slavery controversy.   Monster petitions were sent to Congress praying the adoption of compromise or its submission to the American people before war was started or any other irretrievable step of alienation was taken.   A meeting of Boston workingmen held in Fanueil Hall petitioned as follows:

It is the right of a free people, who are misrepresented and misgoverned by those in power to take counsel together for the redress of their grievances.

The chief cause for the breaking of the Union is the people of the North and the South have been deceived and betrayed by politicians.

The South has been taught to believe that the North hate them and are pledged to trample their rights and property; while the North have been taught to believe that the South hold them in contempt and hatred and are united in a hostile plan of aggression against their liberties.

We plainly see that the ceaseless falsehoods which have misled the South as to our true feelings, and the rash and wicked deeds which are charged upon our whole people, are due to a small but active and unscrupulous party of Abolitionists, who have, etc. . . .

We do earnestly appeal to all patriots, and all honest men at the North to pledge themselves to an unending hostility to the principles and plans of the Abolitionists for the following reasons:

Because they undermine religion and openly deny the authority of the Holy Word of God. . . .

Because the bells of the New England churches which the Abolitionists tolled on the day of the just execution of John Brown, proclaimed their hatred of the Union and their sympathy with his wicked raid and with his murder of peaceable citizens of Virginia.

Because their pretended love of slaves a thousand miles away is but hypocrisy. If they loved mankind and would prevent sin and suffering and wrong, they could find here at home objects more than sufficient for the exercises of all their assumed virtues. But their philanthropy is mere deception, their affected sympathy is selfishness and their feigned love for the slaves a cloak for their insidious designs. . . .

We are weary of the question of slavery; it is a matter which does not concern us, and we wish only to attend to our own business and leave the South to attend to their own affairs, without any interference from the North.

Only in an hour of danger do we step forward to demand and endorse our political rights. And now that we are obliged to come forward for the sake of our country, we learn with profound astonishment from the confession of the great party leaders that the question which divides and distracts the country as to whether slaves shall or shall not be admitted in the territories is a mere quarrel about an abstract opinion; and that in ten years only twelve slaves have been domiciled in the territories in New Mexico. Well may the people say that they must come forward to protect themselves from the politicians.

Let us not quibble about words, or stand obstinately upon slight differences of opinion, like our representatives who dignify their perverse obstinacy with the name of principle, but, disregarding all other objects, unite earnestly, honestly and heartily to preserve the Union.[1]

In fact, petitions, letters, accounts of mass meetings from all parts of the country poured in praying the peaceful preservation of the Union and the avoidance of civil war. Assurances came to Crittenden that the Compromise could be carried by a 50,000 majority in Indiana, by a 200,000 majority in Pennsylvania; that three-fourths of New York were in favor of it: and a petition signed by 22,213 citizens of 182 towns and cities of Massachusetts prayed the adoption of Compromise; 14,000 American women petitioned

---

[1] Crittenden papers, Feb., 1860.

that " party or sectional prejudices be not allowed to prevail over a spirit of mutual conciliation; and one beautiful personal letter to Crittenden closed with " May God in his infinite mercy save the United States of America." [1]

The radical wing of the Republican party which opposed compromise was composed of two groups. One set was for letting the " erring sisters " go in peace. This set was composed of the moral suasionist type of abolitionists [2] and of Horace Greeley, until, as one of the politicians of that day expressd it, Greeley was persuaded to " go the whole soap." [3] This peaceable radical group felt that Civil War was about as bad as slavery, if not worse. The other set in the radical minority wing which Greeley shortly joined was the " war group." [4]   They believed in crushing the secessionists by force of arms and letting the " irrepressible conflict " become

---

[1] Crittenden papers, *passim*, and especially Jay Gould to Crittenden, Jan. 4, 1861.

[2] This was, of course, the doctrine of the *Liberator* and even of the *Springfield* [Mass.] *Republican.* See Nov. 22, 1860. This latter paper regretted the spending of money on arms because it prevented the founding of an agricultural college and aid to Agassiz's Natural History Museum, April 3, 1861.

[3] See Greeley's *American Conflict*, vol. i, p. 359. And for the " whole soap," see Washburne papers, Nat Vose to Washburne, Dec. 15, 1860.

[4] The *Boston Post*, Feb. 9, 1861, contains the following account of the differences between the conservative and radical wing of the party as represented by the conservative *Albany Journal* of Weed and the radical *New York Tribune* of Greeley: " The width of the gulf between the *New York Tribune* and the *Albany Journal* is daily increasing. The *Tribune* intimates that the *Journal* is either traitor or craven; the *Journal* asks how long it is since the *Tribune* insisted on a candidate for President who would not be obnoxious to the Border States. . . . The *Tribune*, in remarking on Seward's declaration that Republicanism must be subordinate to the Union question, declares that it prefers clean Republican principles, *i. e.*, the Chicago platform, to fifty unions; whereupon the *Journal* rejoins that if a choice must be made between party and country, we differ so widely from the *Tribune* as to prefer the Union to fifty parties."

a bloody reality. Lincoln's law partner [1] belonged to this group and it is hardly reasonable to doubt that Lincoln also preferred war to compromise or a dissolution of the Union. The Springfield *State Journal* of Illinois, edited by Lincoln's nephew, was considered an authority on the views of the President-elect. [2] In November, just after the election, it announced the position of Lincoln as being that of his Leavenworth speech which was as follows: "If constitutionally we elect a President and therefore you undertake to destroy the Union, it will be our duty to deal with you as old John Brown was dealt with. We can only do our duty. We hope and believe that in no section will a majority so act as to render such extreme measures necessary." [3]

At no other period in Lincoln's career did he exhibit a more masterful comprehension of the simplicity of the common man's mind than at this crisis. Lincoln skilfully refrained from using the words "civil war," "coercion,"

[1] The following letter from Herndon to Trumbull indicates his position: "This thing slavery must be met and finally squelched. Liberty and slavery are absolute antagonisms: and all human experience and all human philosophy say, 'Clear the ring and let these natural foes, these eternal enemies, now fight it out. To separate them *now* is murderous to the men, women and children of the future. . . . Hurrah for Wade! God bless Wade! . . . We expect you to oppose all the timeserving and cowardly compromise of principle or policy." Trumbull from Herndon, Dec. 21, 1860. Also a letter of Feb. 9, 1861, from Herndon to Trumbull gives the radical point of view: "Are our Republican friends going to concede away dignity, constitutions, union, laws and justice? . . . Before I would buy the South by compromises and concessions to get what is the people's due, I would die to be forgotten, willingly. Let me say to you that if Republicans do concede anything more than the South has already got, namely, her constitutional rights—that you—the Republican party may consider death as the Law."

[2] Washburne papers, Washburne from A. J. Betts, Feb. 4, 1861. "The oft-repeated and emphatic declarations in regard to the position of Mr. Lincoln by the *Springfield Journal* (good authority on that point) I think should set at rest all misgivings as to the course he will pursue."

[3] *Springfield State Journal*, Nov. 14, 1860.

or "subjugation by force of arms" to describe his method for allaying the southern dissatisfaction with northern sectional control of the national government. Instead he chose to call his policy an "enforcement of. the law." In the choice of this phrasing there was a great deal of subtle irony as well as a profound grasp of crowd psychology. The term "enforcement of the law" as it was used in the presidential campaign of 1860 had special reference to the Fugitive Slave Law and the Dred Scott decision of the Supreme Court. The "Union-Savers" strenuously advocated the enforcement of the law, as well as the Douglas Democrats and the Breckinridge party. "Enforcement of the law" had a conservative sound and carried with it an atmosphere of dutiful obedience to law. A great majority clearly favored enforcement of law in general. However, enforcement of the law in connection with the secessionist movement was exactly equivalent to civil war or subjugation by force of arms. A rose by any other name smells as sweet but the use of the words "civil war" would have roused antagonism to the procedure of crushing the secessionists by force of arms while the use of "enforcement of the law" created no such feeling.[1]

Lincoln, it should be carefully noted, did not state publicly that civil war was his chosen policy. In fact one would infer from some of his remarks that peace was his deliberate preference. But it is evident that the "peace" which he preferred and to which he had reference was merely the peace which would have resulted had the southern leaders refrained from challenging a sectional control of the national government and submitted quietly as on normal occasions to the choice of the electoral colleges. However, Lincoln

[1] An excellent account of the magical power of the words is to be found in Le Bon's *The Crowd: A Study of the Popular Mind*, book ii, ch. xi.

refrained from making unequivocally clear to the common man, the difference between the two varieties of "peace." And the common man, with a mind untrained in the critical analysis practiced by lawyers, jumped to the conclusion that there was really no difference between Lincoln's kind of peace and his own. Therefore, the common man approved Lincoln's "peace" policy, because in the excitement of the hour he naïvely mistook it for his own.

When the *Springfield Journal* of March 4, 1861, presented the idea in a most remarkable editorial that a war would put an end to slavery "either in its immediate effects or in the anti-slavery sentiment it would create in all parts of the country," it doubtless gave an excellent clue to what was in the mind of the man who was being inaugurated president of the dis-United States on that day. This editorial seemed to indicate that Lincoln felt that the public opinion of the future could be brought to endorse his war policy and applaud the result provided the first shot in the war was fired by the southerners. Taken as a whole, this editorial may be regarded not only, as a dare, but also, as a warning to the South Carolinians. It is a most marvellously accurate forecast of the future and demonstrates unmistakably Lincoln's clear understanding of the emotions of the common man. However, if such a statement had been officially uttered and explicitly explained by Lincoln, instead of being printed in the newspaper which was understood only by the initiated to represent the President, the common man might have caught on to what the "peace" policy of Lincoln actually amounted to.

That Lincoln was "quite belligerent" seems to have been well understood by those in a position to know.[1] Kreisman, one of the Republican workers among the Ger-

---

[1] Washburne papers, Dec. 27, 1860; Washburne from Kreisman.

mans (who was rewarded for his skill by a secretaryship to the legation at Berlin) wrote Washburne, Republican Congressman from Illinois, that Lincoln had said, "We have plenty of corn and pork, and it would hardly be brave for us to leave this question to be settled by posterity."[1] This news was not intended for public consumption, but was merely a private tip from one good politician to another as to the lay of the land.

The policy which was pursued by the Republican leaders was definitely outlined in a letter from Springfield, Illinois, to Senator Trumbull, who was understood to be Lincoln's spokesman in the United States Senate. It was as follows:[2]

I would then pursue a temporizing policy for the present, keep back out of view our distinctive party principles. Get time for the inauguration, if possible. Then raise the cry of the Constitution and the Union to the exclusion of party principles. Rally all parties under its inspiring influence. Merge all sectional questions into and make them subservient to this plan, and when the smoke of the contest shall have passed away, the Union will be saved, the victory won and our principles secure.

Though this war policy well deserves Francis P. Blair's description of "suaviter in modo, fortiter in re,"[3] it was not one to which the Republican party was pledged by any plank in the Chicago platform except the first clause of the "rotten" plank which was merely a quotation from the Declaration of Independence. It is certain that the vast majority of the northern people who voted for Lincoln did not suspect that they were voting to extend the tenets of the Declaration of

[1] Washburne papers, Dec. 27, 1860; Washburne from Kreisman.

[2] Trumbull papers, Trumbull from Conkling, Dec. 26, 1860. Conkling was one of the party workers who obeyed orders. He wrote a similar letter to Washburne and perhaps to the whole Republican brotherhood in Congress.

Van Buren papers, F. P. Blair to Van Buren, March 7, 1861.

Independence with gunpowder to include the negro slaves in the southern states; for there was another plank in this same platform which expressly declared against such action. In fact, it is absolutely certain that an overwhelming majority of the common American people deliberately opposed engaging in a civil war in any guise to settle the negro question. There is no evidence to indicate that the Republican war group were not aware of this fact. Under the circumstances. there can be no doubt that they knew they had no mandate from the people to settle the negro question for posterity. So much for government of, by and for the people in 1861.

CHAPTER V

THE POLITICAL AND PSYCHOLOGICAL SIGNIFICANCE
OF THE FIRING AT SUMTER

THE wishes of the American people during the months intervening between the secession of South Carolina and the opening guns of the Civil War were very emphatically expressed in every conceivable way. There can be no doubt as to what the American people expressed themselves in favor of during this period; for it stands out very distinctly that they desired the preservation of the Union. Nor can there be any doubt that they preferred the peaceful preservation of the Union to the preservation of the Republican party. The bonds of Union before 1861 were made of the same stuff from which friendships are woven, a light and invisible substance whose texture is finer and more enduring than steel. The bonds of Union previous to 1861 were entwined " with the mystic chords of memory, stretching from every battlefield and patriot grave to every living heart and hearthstone." The vast majority of the Americans manifestly thought that this tried and true method of holding the states together was superior to having the states pinned together by bayonets. Therefore, they favored the adoption of the Crittenden Compromise and the peaceful perpetuation of the Union by methods which were thoroughly in keeping with the principles of a government based on the common consent of the governed in all sections of the country.

However, under the circumstances, a minority of the

northerners felt it was highly desirable for the Federal Government to make an exhibition of its strength to test its power and authority. This minority favored coercing the seceding states. It was composed of persons with strikingly different varieties of motives for their preference for the substitution of force for consent at this crisis, which tested to the uttermost the capacity of the American people of 1860 to measure up to the American people of 1787.

Prominent in this minority were those who were to hold office under the Republican party and who believed that the southern leaders were bluffing to ruin the Republican party. These politicians saw in war the sole means of preserving the public confidence in the Republican leaders. The more astute of them realized that this policy would be preeminently successful only in the event of the secessionists firing the first shot and they, therefore, thought a Fabian policy of delay in announcing a definite decision was advisable on the part of the Republican leaders in order to give the southerners ample time to make this fatal blunder.[1] Then, there were persons who felt that if the Federal Government would show its teeth secession would crumble to dust without much ado.

---

[1] Chase papers, Wright to Chase, March 7, 1861; Brooks to Chase, April 8, 1861; Beckham to Chase, April 2, 1861; Trumbull papers, Trumbull from Plato, March 29, 1861; Trumbull from Judd, Jan. 17, 1861; Van Buren papers, Blair to Van Buren, May 1, 1861, and March 7, 1861; Washburne papers, Washburne from Vose, Dec. 15, 1860: "You are all right in giving the South ample opportunity to remain with decency and to place them fairly and visibly in the wrong before the civilized world," Dec. 18, 1860: "If Mr. Lincoln had sent an armed vessel with provisions for our citizens at Fort Sumter and then if the Rebels had fired upon said ship, we should have a consolidated North," March 16, 1861. Hammond papers, Mallory to Hammond, Dec. 27, 1860. Editorial of Springfield Journal, March 4, 1861. *"Turning on the Light"* by Horatio King, p. 184, "That the first shot in the rebellion came from the enemy was due wholly to this policy of procrastination then so severely censured."

Montgomery Blair, Zachariah Chandler, Carl Schurz and quite a respectable list of northerners followed this school of thought which is, nevertheless, more typical of Prussia than of America.[1]   Some of the coercing minority were convinced that the dignity of the Federal Government would be impaired if the secession theory as a principle of government were tacitly recognized by conciliating the secessionists whom they regarded as attempting to establish the Mexican custom in the United States.[2]   However, a majority of the people, who were utterly opposed to recognizing secession as one of the legal rights of the states, were also opposed to substituting force for consent as the basis of the Union, and therefore favored the adoption of the Crittenden Compromise and an amendment to the Constitution specifically declaring that secession was not one of the rights of a state of the American Union.   Another band of the coercionists, small in number but great in zeal, were those who looked forward to civil war as the means of "melting the chains

[1] *Speeches of Carl Schurz*, edited by himself, p. 32. For Montgomery Blair's views, see Van Buren papers, Blair to Van Buren, April 29, 1861, and Horatio King's *Turning on the Light*, p. 183. For Chandler's position, see Trumbull papers, Chandler to Trumbull, Nov. 17, 1860, and also Chandler to Governor Blair of Michigan, letter of Feb. 11, 1861, in a publication of the Southern Historical Society. Koerner's *Memoirs*, vol. ii, pp. 108-109.

[2] This was the strongest point in the coercionist defense and they stressed it with great force. See the inaugural address of Lincoln and the *New York Tribune's* presentation of the case in the following vein: "The question is simply, Shall the will of the majority, constitutionally and legally expressed at the ballot-box, be respected, or shall we resort to rebellion and civil war whenever we are beaten in an election? Is it possible that the American people will tolerate the introduction of the Mexican system," etc., Jan. 21, 1861; and also the same theme in the *Boston Atlas and Bee* of Feb. 8, 1861, as follows: "We have elected a President strictly according to the provisions of the Constitution and the requirements of the laws of the Union. We have chosen a President after the manner of Washington," etc.

of human bondage."[1] Some of this group of fiery abolitionists were tinged with Brown's fervor, but were without
John Brown's personal courage, for they managed to keep
off the firing line during their holy war.

However, many of the coercionists were doubtless actu-
ated by a varying mixture of the above mentioned motives.
The typical coercionist refused to yield one jot or one tittle of
the Chicago platform as a "matter of conscience." They
were preeminently consistent. But, when one recalls that
what this minority refused to yield as a matter of conscience
was the legal status of negroes in territories which would
never contain the slave system of labor because of the
economic conditions of the territories and that the alterna-
tive to compromise was a dissolution of the Union or civil
war, and when one further considers that under a government of, by and for the people, the will of the majority
should be acceded to, one cannot give these conscientious
Republicans unconditional praise for their strenuous consistency. At this far away day which is witnessing the
dawn of universal peace, the Republican minority appear
a trifle " over-righteous." Moreover, it has now become an
established fact that the actual running of a government
based on the consent of the governed requires that the
political convictions of the minority must never be placed
" beyond doubt, conciliation and compromise."[2]

[1] There were a great many who felt that civil war would end slavery.
See the *Springfield Journal* of March 8, 1861 ; Chase papers, Chase from
Brooks, April 8, 1861 ; Trumbull papers, Herndon to Trumbull, Dec. 21,
1860; Koerner's *Memoirs*, p. 119; Crittenden papers, Salle to Crittenden, Jan. 15, 1861.

[2] Wallas' *Human Nature in Politics*, pp. 194-195. " The most easily
manipulated state in the world would be one inhabited by a race of
non-conformist business men who never followed up a train of political
reasoning in their lives, and who, as soon as they were aware of the
existence of a strong political conviction in their minds, should an-
nounce that it was a matter of conscience, and therefore beyond the
province of doubt and calculation.

Lincoln put the best foot of the coercionist group fore-most[1] in his inaugural address delivered March 4, 1861, upon the occasion of his taking the oath of office to uphold the Constitution of the United States. Jeremiah S. Black had given the Republicans authoritative assurance that, if the Lincoln administration would pledge itself without equivocation to uphold the Constitution of the United States as interpreted by the Supreme Court of the United States, the southern states would annul their ordinances of seces-sion forthwith. The Republicans were asked to make no reference to any special case but only to declare themselves submissive to this legal principle which is the backbone of the American system of government. They flatly refused to make this declaration.[2] A dictum of the Supreme Court had recently declared that slaves were property under the Constitution of the United States and should therefore be recognized as such in the national territories. Under the American system of government as developed by American jurists and statesmen, the decision of the Supreme Court is final until an amendment to the Constitution or another deci-sion of the Court annuls the former decision. Thomas Jef-ferson, Andrew Jackson and Abraham Lincoln are three American presidents who, disagreeing with some particular decision of the Court, have opposed this system; neverthe-less, the system remains intact in spite of the terrific attacks leveled at it by the three distinguished executives. How-ever, the reasoning with which the great chief justice, John Marshall, sustained it in the opinion delivered in the famous case of Marbury *versus* Madison, has never been answered.

In the first inaugural, Lincoln stated that he had the most solemn oath registered in heaven to " preserve, protect and

---

[1] "Coercion," commented the New York *News,* "could not have been put in a more agreeable form; it reads like a challenge under the code."

[2] Black's *Black,* p. 156.

defend the national government " and that to the extent of
his ability he would take care as the Constitution expressly
enjoined him that the laws of the Union be faithfully executed in all the states. He further remarked that the
power confided in him would be used to " hold, occupy and
possess the property and places belonging to the government " and that he would perform this simple duty as far
as practicable, unless his rightful master, the American
people, withheld the requisite means or in some " authoritative " manner directed him otherwise. It should be noted
with what consummate tact Lincoln avoids the unequivocal
declaration that he will support the Constitution of the
United States as interpreted by the Supreme Court and how
gracefully he refrains from obeying the manifest preference
of the American people for conciliation because it had
not been expressed in an " authoritative " manner.

The most vital and important point of the program of
the adminstration which was set forth in the first inaugural,
and upon which the success or failure of the coercionists
depended, consisted in a few apparently simple remarks
addressed evidently to the seceders although there were
none present to profit by them. They were as follows:
" In your hands, my dissatisfied fellow-countrymen, and
not in mine, is the momentous issue of civil war. The Government will not assail you. You can have no conflict without being yourselves the aggressors." Manifestly, there
was one point on which Mr. Lincoln had become absolutely
convinced and that was that it would be extremely unwise
for the coercionist minority to undertake to coerce the seceding states unless it appeared that the undertaking was in
self-defense. He felt, in company with other astute coercionists, that they could not afford to fire the first shot in
the opening of hostilities. The public opinion of America
would not sanction the adoption of force *per se* until it

was certain that conciliation had failed and it is extremely doubtful whether it would have adopted it then. For the " let the erring sisters go in peace " of the *bona fide* abolitionists had a backing outside of the abolitionist circle and the secessionists *per se* very strongly advocated this same policy. Lincoln's insistence upon the South's being the aggressor (he made this assertion both in his inaugural and in his public utterances on his way to Washington from Springfield for the inauguration) and the insistence upon this point by the members of Lincoln's cabinet and by the Republican coercionist press during this period, shows conclusively that Lincoln and the Republican coercionists accurately gauged the public opinion of the time.[1]   The tremendous signifi-

[1] Speech at Philadelphia and Indianapolis on his way to Washington and *Springfield Journal* of March 4 and March 7, 1861 ; the New Haven [Conn.] *Journal and Courier* of April 11, after the expedition had been sent to Sumter, solemnly assured its readers that " In these movements the Administration is not provoking rebellion or war. It is simply sustaining the Constitution and preserving the authority of the State. If any attack is made it will be an overt act of resistance to the United States, an act of treason, calling for all the power of the Government to put it down. There is Fort Sumter with a United States garrison. Its garrison needs provisions and it is the duty of the Government to furnish them. If interfered with, it must use force against force. Perhaps ere this, force has been applied, and maybe the telegraph this morning will bring accounts of actual acts of treason. The people are true to the core and will fully sustain the Government in preserving its honor, and its very existence." The *New York Evening Post* of April 9, 1861, contains the following cloudy treatment of the inauguration of the coercion policy in an editorial entitled " Bow-wow !": " How the Charlestonians will fight, after so many weeks of savage preparation and more savage boasting, remains to be discovered. But no one will deny them the credit of being most persistent and ingenious bullies. They have bullied everybody and every side for now some five months. . . . We have been bullied with pictures of the horrors of bloodshed— we have been bullied with descriptions of the pleasures of peace—our Charleston fellow-citizens (for they are yet citizens of the United States, in spite of themselves) have threatened to starve us ; to draw all the coin of the North to the South ; to send us not a bale of cotton— they have threatened to do everything but eat Major Anderson and his

cance of " Who fired the first shot?" to the common man,
was brought out continually during the whole war, when
northern prisoners upon being reproached for fighting to
"make niggers the equal of white men," would repeatedly
defend themselves by retorting, " Who fired the first shot? "

In view of the fact that three-fifths of the American
people voted against Lincoln, and that probably more than
four-fifths of the American people preferred compromise to
civil war or to a dissolution of the Union, it is important
to note that Lincoln based his attack upon secession and
his refusal to acknowledge it as one of the rights of a
state upon the fact that the secessionists were not a majority but a minority of the American people. " If the minority," he said, "will not acquiesce, the majority must,
or the government must cease. There is no other alterna-
tive; for continuing the government is acquiescence on one
side or the other. If a minority in such case secede rather
than acquiesce they make a precedent which in turn will

men, and we have no doubt they would threaten that if they thought it
would scare the brave major. Like veritable bullies, they have endeav-
ored to achieve by loud talking what men very seldom achieve without
hard blows. They have roared like lions, and they have a right to feel
hurt that no one seems alarmed.

" There is an old fable of a lion and a donkey going hunting in company. Coming to a cave in which were some goats, the donkey volun-
teered to enter and by his brays frighten out the goats, who would thus
rush into the lion's mouth. The donkey, knowing the harmless nature
of the goats, rushed in and alarmed them with most terrific roars.
After which, emerging, half out of breath, he found his companions
surrounded by carcasses. ' Did I not roar terribly?' said the vain donkey, anxious to elicit a compliment. ' You did,' gravely replied the lion;
' I should have been frightened myself if I had not known who it was.'

" Among the telegraphic messages received here from Charleston yesterday is one which has a most horrid and frightful roar:

" ' Bloodshed is inevitable, and if one drop of blood is spilt, no one
knows when it will end.'

" We should be very much frightened at this—only we know who it
is. It is only a South Carolina donkey."

divide and ruin them: for a minority of their own will secede from them whenever a majority refuses to be controlled by such a minority."

This is a very accurate statement. A majority had voted against Lincoln and a majority of the nation wanted compromise, while Lincoln, representing a minority, refused to accede to the wishes of the majority. It was perfectly true that the majority of the nation were opposed to secession or the breaking up of the nation, but they were in favor of preserving the national unity, not by war but by the time-honored method of conciliation. It is highly probable that a majority of American voters believed that Lincoln's above statement applied solely to the secessionist *per se* minority— because a majority of American voters did not know then, and do not know now, that a man can be legally elected President when a vast majority have voted against him.[1]

Lincoln also refrained in the inaugural from referring to the doctrines enunciated in the House-Divided speech and confined his anti-slavery doctrines to the single statement that the only substantial difference between the sections was that one section thought slavery was right and ought to be extended and that the other thought it was wrong and ought not to be extended. This reduction of the anti-slavery tenets of the Republican party to a false simplicity was thoroughly in keeping with the plan outlined in the letter to Trumbull which advised " keeping back out of view our distinctive party principles." The slavery question at that time was hardly a simple matter of right and wrong and certainly it is incorrect to infer that the inaugural treated it as such; for the treatment of the negro question in the inaugural is distinctly political rather than moral. The question was then and is now fundamentally a racial question, although at that time its political importance was paramount. It

---

[1] Hence it is possible " to fool some of the people all of the time."

also had its social, economic and legal phases, all of which Mr. Lincoln subordinated to the exigency of maintaining the public confidence in his leadership. The maintenance of the public's confidence necessitates that a leader should never obviously back down from a position he has definitely upheld.

Another prominent feature of the inaugural was the incorporation of the Rev. R. J. Breckinridge's theory of national supremacy. It is interesting to note that this famous theory of national supremacy derives one supreme nation from the thirteen (or thirty-three) sovereign states of the Union by a logical process similar to that by which the Geneva Catechism establishes the Calvinistic doctrine of the Trinity. The Rev. Dr. Breckinridge was a learned Presbyterian theologian and wielded great influence not only in Kentucky[1] but also in Missouri where his nephew, Judge Samuel Miller Breckinridge, influenced the Missourians to act on his advice. The address which contained the national supremacy theory had had a much wider circulation than the two above mentioned border states. It was delivered on Jan. 4, 1861, at Lexington, Ky. and immediately attracted attention all over the United States. It was published in the newspapers, went through several pamphlet editions and was even published in the London Times.[3] President Lincoln evidently found it highly

[1] Breckinridge papers, R. J. Breckinridge to W. C. P. Breckinridge, Jan., 1861, and Garret Davis to R. J. Breckinridge, Jan. 19, 1861.

[2] *Ibid.*, see letters of S. M. Breckinridge to R. J. Breckinridge in the first months of 1861 down through April 8.

[3] *Ibid.* Letters came to the Rev. R. J. Breckinridge from all over the country. See especially letters dated Jan. 15, 16, Feb. 17, Feb. 22; W. M. Hill of Louisville, who apparently had in charge the distribution of the pamphlet edition, writes that there were " many calls for speech of Jan. 4 from the North but very few from the South." However, see Breckinridge papers, *passim*, for the extent of circulation of the so-called " Fast Day Sermon."

useful; for, he used its arguments not only in the first inaugural but also in his first message to Congress.[1]

The major thesis of the first inaugural seemed to be that there was but one course which stern duty left open for the administration and that the dutiful President would unflinchingly take that course. However, the President warily added that "the course here indicated will be followed unless current events and experience shall show a modification or change to be proper and in every case and exigency my best discretion will be exercised according to circumstances actually existing, and with a view and hope of a peaceful solution of the national troubles and the restoration of fraternal sympathies and affections."

After reading the inaugural, Elmer Wright of Boston wrote Salmon P. Chase that it was " the most masterly piece of generalship which human history has yet to show" within his knowledge. " I hardly know," he continued, "which most to admire, the adroit and effective use of the rotten plank in the Chicago platform or the sound judgment which puts the supreme court back in its proper place. The whole drift shows that the new president's heart is in the right place [with the radicals of the North], and that though far in advance of the average North — he knows how to make it follow him solid. My only hope for the country has long been the folly of the slaveholders. That does not seem likely to fail now. The wiser and kinder you are, the more foolish they will be, and the surer to fight and be destroyed."[2]

[1] *Ibid.* Happersett to R. J. B., Sept. 13, 1861. " He [Lincoln] evidently wanted to see you and spoke in highest terms of you. I regret that you did not visit Washington. I alluded to your article on the state of the country as being entirely the most satisfactory and conclusive on that subject of all that had been written. He seemed familiar with it, as I supposed he was from his message to Congress. That whole argument about state sovereignty, *etc.*, was yours. He is your *warm* friend. . . . The truth is we are looking to you for the support of Ky. to the General Government more than to any living man."

[2] Chase papers, Wright to Chase, March 7, 1861.

The inaugural was indeed a masterpiece of its kind.   Its emphasis on the perpetuity of the Union and its reduction of the obnoxious anti-slavery doctrine of the Chicago platform to a mere matter of opinion on the right and wrong of slavery with no program apparently attached for enforcing the northern view, did not unnecessarily or prematurely alarm the Union-Savers of the border slave states. These states impatiently awaited, but awaited, to see if the current of events would not modify the coercionist course indicated in the inaugural.   The North was well satisfied. There was nothing in it to agitate excessively the conservatives who approved of the idea of the " enforcement of the law," while at the same time, there was enough nourishment in the " enforcement of the law " for the war group.   The seceded South saw nothing but war in it, for it very emphatically repudiated a peaceful dissolution of the Union and offered no apology for the sectionalization of the national government.   It contained nothing which limited the years of control by the northern sectional league. The inaugural reveals the truth that Lincoln was no " Simple Susan," but as shrewd a Yankee as America has ever produced.[1]   Many of the border states people seem to have felt, that the revealed policy of Lincoln later proved him to be a guilty dissembler in the inaugural.   However, he was skillfully accurate but it was impossible for the common man, with his mind untrained in the critical analysis practiced by lawyers and politicians to grasp the full significance of his statement.   Elmer Wrights were relatively very few.

Nothing more clearly brings out the essential difference between the statesmanship of Clay and Lincoln than a comparison of their tactics on like occasions, when the main point of dispute between the North and the South was over

[1] See Lamon's *Lincoln* for substantiation of this, p. 481.

the legal status of the negro though this was, on both occasions, a matter of no practical importance in itself. Clay
was able on the occasion of the admission of Missouri to
the Union to persuade the "conscientious" northerner to
forego his conscientious litigiousness for the sake of peace.
"What is your plan," Clay asked the northerners, "in
regard to Missouri?" Do you intend to coerce her to alter
her Constitution? How will you do all this? Is it your
design to employ the bayonet? We tell you frankly our
views. They are to admit her absolutely if we can, and, if
not, with the condition which we have offered. You are
bound to disclose your views with equal frankness. You
aspire to be thought statesmen. As sagacious and enlightened statesmen, you should look to the fearful future, and
let the country understand what is your remedy for the
evils which lie before us." [1] The northern leaders of that
day had no plan for the fearful future and acceded to the
compromise. But the northern anti-slavery leaders of 1860
had two plans, one of which was to let the "erring sisters"
go in peace. The other plan, which was advocated by the
coercionists, was accurately, but not frankly and explicitly
laid before the American people in the inaugural address
of Lincoln. However, it was completely outlined in the
Trumbull letter from Springfield, which advocated merg-
ing all sectional questions into and making them subservient
to forceful preservation of the Union and "when the smoke
of battle shall have passed away, the Union will be saved,
the victory won, and our principles secure." Whether Lincoln originated this plan is immaterial. The main point is
he carried it out.

Before the Republican accession to office, the Republican
leaders were very anxious for President Buchanan to take
summary proceedings against South Carolina after the

[1] Prentice's *Clay*, pp. 208-209.

fashion of Andrew Jackson. But James Buchanan was not molded on the lines of Andrew Jackson, for Buchanan was not cursed or blessed with the ability to see only one side of a question. (As a northerner, he understood the northern point of view but he tried so hard to be fair to the extreme southerners during his entire administration that the northerners came to feel that he resembled the man who thanked the beggar to whom he had just given alms). The Republicans felt that if the Democratic president took prompt action to crush secession in South Carolina, none of the other southern states would have dared secede, no matter how pat the Republicans stood on the Chicago platform nor how tightly they held to the propriety of the sectional control of the national government. But Buchanan was unable to conclude that the situation of 1860 was sufficiently like that of 1832 to justify the same treatment. He felt that there were more differences than likenesses between 1832 and 1860. It was obvious that South Carolina was the storm center on both occasions but the likeness stopped about there. The situation of 1860 was more serious than that of 1832 for two reasons. First: The numbers of persons feeling dissatisfaction were vastly greater in 1860 than in 1832 and the whole South and not one state was involved. Second: The intensity of the feeling of dissatisfaction of 1860 was vastly deeper than in 1832. It so happens that the difference between a mob revolt and a respectable revolution is only a matter of numbers and intensity. Therefore, Buchanan concluded that 1860 should not be handled like 1832. He favored the adoption of the Crittenden Compromise and used, as a result of his principles, the utmost care to prevent a clash between the federal and state authorities—without, at the same time, recognizing the right of secession. He thus kept the road clear for a peaceful solution of the controversy by the incoming administration, the personnel of which he thought responsible for the crisis because of the attempted sectional control of the government. Lincoln had sowed the wind in the House-Divided speech and Buchanan was willing to do nothing which would keep the Republican President from reaping his own whirlwind.[1] Before condemning Buchanan for not adopting the policy in regard to South Carolina so highly recommended by the Republican leaders, it should be recalled that Buchanan accurately represented the will of the majority of the American people which was in favor of a peaceful preservation of the Union. And if obedience to the will of the majority of the people can be taken as a criterion of merit under a government of, by and for the people, then Buchanan deserves praise for his careful performance of duty during the last four months of his administration. Buchanan so acted that he neither made civil war inevitable, nor a successful dissolution of the Union possible.[1] He neither followed the advice of the Republican leaders who wished him to heavily garrison all of the southern forts, including Fort Sumter, nor the advice of the secessionists *per se* who desired him to evacuate the forts and recognize the dissolution of the Union.[2] He acted under the advice of Jeremiah S. Black, one of the ablest jurists America has yet produced.

It is a tremendously serious responsibility to take the decisive step which turns loose the dogs of war, and especially the dogs of civil war. After being inaugurated, the Republicans apparently hesitated to send reënforcements to the federal garrisons located in the southern states.

[1] See letter of Joseph Holt to James O. Harrison, Jan. 14, 1861, in James O. Harrison papers, and letter of J. S. Black to James Buchanan, Oct. 5, 1861, in Black papers for an understanding of this position. Also see Black's instructions to foreign ministers in Black papers.

[2] Trescot's account, edited by Gaillard Hunt.

The garrison at Fort Sumter lying in Charleston Harbor, South Carolina, was the cynosure of all eyes. The fact that it was in the home state of the secessionists *per se* created a very critical situation, for the secessionists had demanded its surrender to the state authorities. The secessionists *per se* had been prevailed upon in the interests of a peaceable secession to await decisive action on the part of the incoming administration before reducing the fort. President Lincoln sent a special messenger to South Carolina to report to him the exact state of feeling in this locality, and he seems to have faithfully reported the condition existing.[1]   Given the acute state of feeling in South Carolina, it was thoroughly understood that an attempt by the Republicans to reënforce either with arms or provisions the garrison at Fort Sumter would result in the South Carolinians opening fire on the American flag—the flag which had ceased to represent for them a government based on the consent of the governed. The South Carolinians judged that an attempt on the part of the Republican administration to reënforce the federal forts in the southern seceded states would be undeniable evidence that the Republicans had decided on coercion unless such action was preceded by a compromise agreement. The South Carolinians felt that an attempt to coerce the seceded states would bring the entire South to their side [2] and that the policy of coercion of the Republicans would not be sustained by a united North; for before the reënforcement of Sumter there were three well defined groups in the North, namely, the coercionists, the conciliating Unionists, and the peaceful dissolutionists.

The people of the northern tier of slave states were unanimously in favor of a peaceful perpetuation of the Union provided the Lincoln administration gave evidence

[1] Lamon's *Lincoln*, p. 79.
[2] Crawford papers, F. W. Pickens to Toombs, Feb. 12, 1861.

of conciliation. They were unanimously in favor of peaceful adjustment and unanimously opposed to coercion. The inaugural had not closed the door completely on conciliation, and the border people anxiously awaited decisive action on the part of the administration. They implored the evacuation of Fort Sumter by the Federal Government on the ground of giving the South Carolinians a good opportunity to cool down before the difficulty was pushed to a bloody extreme.[1] If there was ever a people who more earnestly desired peace than the inhabitants of the border states their prayers are not recorded. The border state leaders seemed to have fully realized that the disunionists *per se* were increasing in numbers and that the war party at the North was also gaining recruits as the news of the radical disunionist *per se* utterances were circulated broadcast at the North by the northern radical papers. The border states people felt that if a collision between the two sets of radicals could be indefinitely delayed, both groups would perish from peace. They knew that the conciliatory unionists were in a majority. William H. Seward, Lincoln's Secretary of State, gave heed to their prayers in regard to the evacuation of Fort Sumter and even for a time thought that he had convinced or could convince Lincoln that this was a desirable course.[2] He led the southern commissioners

---

[1] Letter of John M. Harlan, typical view of border statesmen. Holt papers, Harlan to Holt, March 11, 1861. Also see in Breckinridge papers, letter of James O. Harrison to W. C. P. Breckinridge, March 30, 1861.

[2] There has been some dispute in regard to whether Seward acted with Lincoln's knowledge in his communication with the southern commissioners. Lincoln was too shrewd to commit himself definitely but it is highly probable that Lincoln consented to the circulation of the report that Sumter was to be evacuated for the purpose of conciliating the peace faction in the Republican party which Seward represented. See the account of Seward's policy given in the *Springfield Journal*, March 15, 1861. The Republican press announced that if the Repub-

who were negotiating the recognition of the southern Confederacy at Washington to believe that Sumter would be evacuated and they were asked to wait until after the policy of evacuation could be tried out in the North.[1]

The report that Sumter was to be evacuated was accordingly circulated throughout the North.[2] This experiment was to test out whether a " peace policy " on the part of the administration would hold the alienated conservative element in the ranks of the Republican party. Local and congressional elections were to take place in Connecticut, Rhode Island, Ohio, and a few other places, during the last of March and the first of April. The candidates opposing the Republican nominees in these elections ran on the fusion ticket now completely fused and known as " Unionists " or "Union Democrats," the name of " Union-Saver" being now no longer a matter of open derision. It was apparent that the mass of the people began to feel that, after all, the " old gentlemen " who launched the Union party the year before did understand the signs of the times. The " Unionist" press of the North assisted by the Democrats, chorused " We told you what the election of a sectional president would result in."

licans won the spring elections it would mean peace. Doubtless this was perfectly true, but many conservative Republicans did not see the point and obdurately voted for the Union-Democrats, who also promised peace.

[1] The Confederate commissioners were commended by the Secretary of State of the Confederate States for their conduct in suspending a demand for a reply in order to enable the Government of the United States to ascertain the effect of the evacuation of Fort Sumter. Date of commendatory letter, March 28, 1861, Crawford papers.

[2] The *New York Tribune* report of the evacuation closed with the following: " Let all remember that the strength has not yet departed from our flag and that this movement (evacuation of Sumter) may be only the crouch to precede the decisive leap." Greeley was on the " inside" at this period and knew perfectly well what the situation was in the cabinet, and in the White House.

The spring elections unmistakably showed the trend of public opinion. A reaction against the Republicans had set in and the result was pretty much of a landslide for the Union-Democrats. Cincinnati went fusionist by a good majority; Sandusky, Cleveland, Toledo, Columbus and other cities lined up behind the "dough-face" opposition as the radical wing of the Republican party was pleased to call those who did not see through radical spectacles. Even Republican New England broke ranks in spots. It looked as though the Republican party were breathing its last and were being consigned to oblivion for bringing on a dissolution of the Union. Nobody was quite so unpopular at this period as an abolitionist.

It was clear to Seward on April 1, when the returns from the elections held the last of March had come in, that the country was clamoring for peace and the only possible way to preserve peace was to evacuate Fort Sumter. He doubtless felt that the mere report that Sumter was to be evacuated was not sufficient to win anew the alienated conservative vote which the Administration's not-an-inch policy in regard to compromise had turned away from allegiance to Republicanism. So, he wrote Lincoln a note, bearing the date April 1, (and some have thought it very appropriately dated), which has become quite famous. In this note he offered to take the responsibility—manifestly, for the evacuation of Fort Sumter. It seems that Seward, the author of the "irrepressible conflict" phrase, really had no desire for the conflict to become a reality especially while his constituents were clamoring for peace. In the face of a landslide for the Union-Democrats, it seems possible that Seward might have been nervous over his political future on April 1, 1861. But Lincoln calmly replied that he was willing to take the responsibility—manifestly, for Civil War, although one might infer that he was willing to share this responsibility, because he was careful to ask his cabinet to hand him their opinions in regard to Fort Sumter in writing, on March 15, and again on March 29, Judging from these written replies to the President's requests, the question which troubled the cabinet was not so much whether Fort Sumter should or should not be evacuated. but was whether the country—the common man—would or would not come to the conclusion that the Republican leaders were responsible for the Civil War which it was felt that the reënforcement of Sumter would precipitate.[1]

Francis P. Blair, Sr, and other members of the coercionist group protested vigorously when they heard it rumored that Sumter was to be evacuated. In fact many members of the war group were disgusted at Mr. Lincoln's way of " putting his foot down." [2] The Secretary of the Treasury, who was a member of this group on the " inside," doubtless considerably relieved the minds of some of his radical supporters when he wrote them as follows:[3]

Gentlemen: It is so natural for Republicans to be in opposition to the administration at Washington that they do not as yet realize the necessity of defending its measures as a matter of duty, relying on the President and his Cabinet to be true to their principles when their policy by force of circumstances is concealed from the public view or must of necessity for a time remain undisclosed. I greatly regret the result of the election in our State from causes so utterly beyond all control.

The " necessity " or " force of circumstances " which for a time caused the policy of the Lincoln administration to remain undisclosed or concealed from public view was of two

---

[1] Nicolay and Hay, *Complete Works of Abraham Lincoln*, vol. vi.

[2] Van Buren papers, Blair to Van Buren, May 1, 1861. Trumbull papers, Plato to Trumbull, March 29, 1861. Chase papers, Antrams to Chase, 1861.

[3] Chase papers, Chase to Antrams, April 9, 1861.

varieties.   The announcement that Sumter was to be evacuated and the delay in sending support to Sumter until after
the effect of a " peace policy " on the Republican party fortunes could be demonstrated for Seward's benefit, was doubtless a compromise arrangement by which neither wing of
the Republican party was alienated.   An announcement
on March 4 that the administration definitely intended to reënforce Sumter would have alienated the conservatives.
That Seward did not resign from the cabinet when the
" stirring up of Sumter " was finally decided upon indicates
the efficacy of the delay.   And furthermore, if " bread "
was not sent to Sumter until the garrison was actually in
need the common man would be much more likely to feel that
the Federal Government was not " coercing " the seceded
states.   Manifestly, the Administration was awaiting the
" psychological moment " and it had arrived when on April
8, one of the Confederate commissioners at Washington received the following telegram from Charleston signed by
General Beauregard: " Special messenger from Lincoln
Mr. Chew informs us Sumter to be provisioned peaceably,
otherwise forcibly."

As the ships bearing supplies sent by the Lincoln administration appeared on the horizon outside of the Charleston harbor, the South Carolinians opened fire from the
batteries on the shore of the harbor.   There was no possible
chance of holding the fort by the Federal authorities, but
as Horace White has so well said, " Nothing could have
been contrived so sure to awaken the volcanic forces that
ended in the destruction of slavery as the spectacle in
Charleston Harbor." [1]   Blair hoped that the spirit of patriotism would be aroused in the northern people by the
fort's being lost by battle rather than by tame evacuation.[2]

[1] *Lyman Trumbull*, by Horace White, p. 164.
[2] Van Buren papers, Van Buren from Blair, May 1, 1861.

The lowering of the American flag which accompanied the surrender of the fort to the South Carolinians unified the North, the people of which locality proceeded to stand together regardless of party political differences on the " platform of the flag." And Lincoln contentedly wrote to the commander of the Sumter expedition that even though the fort was lost the purpose of the expedition was accomplished.[1] The South Carolinians had not profited sufficiently by the advice in the inaugural, i.e., " You can have no conflict without yourselves being the aggressors." Upon the fall of Sumter, Lincoln issued forthwith a call for 75,000 troops to defend the government and put down the traitorous insurrection. Thus was the policy of coercion formally declared. The delay in revealing it had been one of purposeful indecision, for the result was a united North. But there is no evidence to indicate that the thousands of northern men who sanctioned the call to arms issued by the President had any desire to abolish slavery by the sword or that they had any intention to deny the southerners one iota of their rights under a government based on the " common" consent of the governed. They merely felt an over-

[1] Nicolay and Hay, *Complete Works of Abraham Lincoln*, vol. vi, pp. 261-262; A. Lincoln to Gustavus V. Fox, May 1, 1861, " You and I both anticipated that the cause of the country would be advanced by making the attempt to provision Fort Sumter, even if it should fail; and it is no small consolation now to feel that our anticipation is justified by the result." It was very easy for the Republicans to get the preservation of the Republican party mixed up with the preservation of the Union. They considered the two, one and inseparable. See Tyler papers, John Tyler to Benj. Patton, May 7, 1861, for Tyler's view of Lincoln's action, " Who can fail to acknowledge that the demonstration on Ft. Sumter was a mere pretext for what followed. The stake played for is neither to repair his own wounded honor or to avenge the flag which he purposely designed to be struck from the flagstaff of Ft. Sumter, but to rally the masses of the North around his own person and to prevent the faction which had brought him into power from falling asunder. In this he has succeeded."

whelming desire to defend the flag, the sacred symbol of free government, from desecration. The popularity of

> " Shoot if you must this old grey head,
>   But spare your country's flag, she said,"

is very significant. It is not an accident that the "Star Spangled Banner " is the national anthem of America. The flag is far more reverenced in the " land of the free and the home of the brave " than the President, for the flag can do no wrong. The Americans are said to have a " bunting patriotism " because it is so easily aroused by a combination of " red white and blue " bunting. This feeling is especially noticeable in Americans in foreign lands when they see the stars and stripes floating in the breeze.[1]

The enormous difference made by the manner in which coercion was put into effect is a matter of great psychological interest. The change in public sentiment in the northerners produced by the incidents connected with the firing on the flag in Charleston Harbor seemed almost miraculous to some of the Republicans. Instead of a minority, the coercionists suddenly became a majority as if by magic.[2] The

---

[1] The following quotation from a letter in the Manuscripts Division of the Library of Congress, from a man in Philadelphia to " Charlie" [dated April 15, 1861] illustrates the flag sentiment in the North: " Great guns, never saw such excitement, people crazy, large crowds of boys and young men of the lowest class running through the city making rum mills and taverns throw out the stars and stripes to the breeze to satisfy their union sentiments, consequently the town is filled with the National Bunting. . . . I expect from the universal excitement that 75,000,000 to 100,000,000 men will call to see the C. S. A. shortly. Everybody is for going down to conquer the rebels."

[2] The evidence that a great change was produced by the firing on the flag at Sumter upon the public opinion at the North is overwhelming. See Greeley's *American Conflict*, vol. i, p. 458; Chase papers, Nash to Chase, May 3, 1861, " I would not have believed that such a change in public opinion could have occurred in so short a time." Mitchell to Chase, April 18, 1861, " The change in public sentiment is wonderful—

law of the mental unity of crowds went into effect with the firing on the flag at Sumter and the call to arms. The mental phenomenon produced by these events is one of common occurrence on a small scale but seldom has it been demonstrated in such vast proportions.

The psychological explanation of what happened is as follows: In addition to the excitemtnt of the instinct of counter-attack,[1] which is one of man's most powerful instincts, the northern people found themselves reaching the conclusion that the whole South was responsible for the firing on Sumter, instead of the relatively small group of secessionists *per se*. The excitement of the public mind caused by a presidential election had been continued by the secession of the southern peoples and was raised to a high state of expectancy by the announcement in the newspapers

almost miraculous — a few weeks since the leading commercial paper here, and a very influential one in mercantile circles, the *Journal of Commerce*, to prevent the spreading of Republican sentiments, announced that the prominent advocate thereof would be the first to be visited by public condemnation should hostilities commence. Instead, *vice versa*." Ball to Chase, April 16, 1861, "There's nothing but force to bring the rebels to reason. Mr. Lincoln's proclamation has reached the heart of our whole people and they are now organizing for the conflict." Archibald to Chase, April 24, 1861, "You have no doubt noticed the astonishing outbreak of patriotic enthusiasm in the newspapers since the firm stand by the Administration in the controversy with the Algerine Confederacy. . . . The loyal enthusiasm of the People cannot be overstated or exaggerated. . . . Lincoln stock arose one thousand per cent at least and if the spring elections were to come off now the result would be very different. Courage and intrepidity win all." Hammond papers, R. Buchanan to Hammond, April 17, 1861, "The Fort Sumter affair united the entire North and West to sustain the honor of our flag and uniform and the integrity of the Union at all hazards." Washburne papers, April 15, 1861, Wheeler to Washburne, "The change in sentiment here in the last ten days is most wonderful— all say the Government must be sustained."

[1] See Thorndike's *Educational Psychology*, p. 24, for a description of this instinct.

that Fort Sumter was to be provisioned. This abnormal condition of the public brain was that which the psychologist terms a " suggestible state of mind." Psychologically speaking, a " suggestion " is a process of communication resulting in the acceptance with conviction of the communicated proposition in the absence of logically adequate grounds for its acceptance. The impressive character of the source from which the suggestion is communicated enhances the amount of illogicalness which the " suggestible " brain will pass by without question in accepting the suggested proposition with the utmost conviction. A deficiency of knowledge relating to the topic in regard to which the suggestion is made also increases the chances for the suggestion to take effect.[1]

A deficiency of knowledge existed in the North in regard to the cause of secession, especially among that portion of the electorate whose reading was confined to the Republican partisan press, and the response to the call to arms had to be made with such rapidity that there was no time to investigate adequately who ordered the firing on the flag, and to discover that the situation after the firing was the same in so far as the mass of southern people were concerned as before the firing. The suggestion which came from the President of the United States was that " a lawless combination " of persons was attacking the Federal Government and the nation, and that this combination must be suppressed if government based on the consent of the governed was to be perpetuated in the United States. The northern people accepted this suggestion with conviction and rushed to arms. Argument was silenced and reason dethroned and the non-rational inference held sway throughout the nation.

[1] See McDougall's *Social Psychology* for an account of the " suggestion," pp. 96-102.

In the southern states, the calling out of 75,000 troops by Lincoln had the same effect on the southern people as the firing on the flag had produced in the North. The law of the mental unity of crowds went into effect[1] and great numbers of southern people who had voted for Douglas and Bell and who conceded that South Carolina had no business to fire on the flag, rushed to arms to prevent the establishment of a government based on force in the southern states. It was felt that the call for troops by the Black Republican President was the final proof of the hostile intentions toward the South first enunciated in the House-Divided speech. Virginia, Arkansas, Tennessee and North Carolina swiftly dashed out of the Union and the other border slave states almost dashed away also. " Maryland, My Maryland "[2] was roughly bridled—which is to say that President Lincoln had a number of the leading Marylanders jailed without benefit of the writ of *habeas corpus* to prevent them from taking Maryland formally out of the Union. The South was convinced that the " despot's heel " was on her shores and that the common defense needed providing for against the Republican regime.

Considering the convictions of both northerners and southerners, the battle cry of " Freedom " was equally appropriate for both northern and southern armies. But the freedom envisaged by both northerner and southerner was the freedom of the white man and not the freedom of the

---

[1] Le Bon's *The Crowd*, bk. I, ch. I.

[2] " Dear mother, burst the tyrant's chain,
    Maryland!
Virginia should not call in vain,
    Maryland!
She meets her sisters on the plain:
' *Sic semper* ' 'tis the proud refrain,
That baffles minions back amain—
    Maryland, my Maryland."

African slaves.   Both the North and the South were willing to suffer to the uttermost to perpetuate and preserve " government based on consent."   The northerner looked upon secession and the firing on the flag as attempts on the part of the southerners to destroy that kind of government; while the southerners looked upon a northern sectional president summoning to arms 75,000 troops as an attempt to sub-jugate the South and annihilate the fundamental basis of a government of, by and for the people in the southern states.

Certainly there is no evidence that the war which followed was an " irrepressible conflict " between free and slave labor.   It was, however, a definite failure of democratic government to meet an emergency created primarily by the election of a sectional president according to the letter of the Constitution.   Such an election defeated one of the primary purposes of the Constitution which was " to insure domestic tranquility." [1]   Civil War is in itself the reverse of " domestic tranquility."   It seems highly probable that the Constitution would have been equal to this crisis, had not the presidential election machinery been subverted by political parties, or had Washington's advice regarding the formation of geographical political parties been incorporated in the Constitution in the form of an amendment requiring the president to have in addition to the other requirements, at least 3 per cent of the popular vote in every state of the Union.   However, Lincoln felt that 10 per cent of the voting population in 1860 would be necessary to reestablish the Federal authority in a seceded state. [2]   But 3 per cent of the voters would insure that the national policy had something in common with every state.

[1] The preamble of the Constitution of the United States gives the purposes for which it was established.

[2] Lincoln's Amnesty Proclamation, Dec. 8, 1863.

CHAPTER VI

KENTUCKY'S DECISION

THE great problem common to all of the border slave states upon the inauguration of Civil War was merely a matter of the side they were to stand by and fight on in the battles destined to be fought on their own soil. It was no easy problem to solve. Needless to say civil war which might bring servile insurrection into their midst was not of their choosing. In order to bring the border-state conditions in general into the spotlight, it has seemed desirable to concentrate attention on Kentucky, one of the northern tier of border states and the most centrally located of them. For, Kentucky was not only a typical border slave state but also became a pivotal state—so great was the importance of her decision.

The Kentuckians of today have a reputation for being too ready with the use of fire-arms, but the Kentuckians of 1861 were the most peaceable of all Americans. Civil war meant for them the direst of calamities, calamities from which they have not recovered after the lapse of over half a century.[1] Kentucky's 700 miles of defenseless and

[1] The greatest calamity was the debasement of political morality which was brought about by the injection of a mass of totally ignorant negroes into the electorate. These voters are gradually becoming more intelligent, but the mass of them still vote solidly the Republican ticket without the slightest knowledge of the questions involved in the election. They do so in childlike gratitude to Abraham Lincoln, who, they are constantly reminded, was their great benefactor. One wonders how they would vote if they knew that Lincoln wanted them all shipped out of the country back to Africa after he had gotten them freed.

indefensible frontier along the Ohio River offered no inducement to her inhabitants to go to war with the inhabitants of the three populous states of Ohio, Indiana and Illinois, just across the river.   On this line where the free and slave states met there was no " irrepressible conflict " visible; in fact the inhabitants of the states on either side of the Ohio River were on the friendliest of terms.   So friendly were they that at the time Sumter fell, Kentucky had hardly enough gunpowder within her borders to fire a Fourth of July salute.   Kentucky had been called the dark and bloody ground in the Indian days, but she had no desire to have her soil experience a second immersion as the battle ground of the sections.   It should hardly be a matter of surprise that every Kentuckian, including John C. Breckinridge, was absolutely opposed to civil war as the means of settling the difference of opinion between the North and the South in regard to what constituted a sectional control of the national government.   Kentucky felt that if the leaders of both extremes had consulted either the interests or the counsels of Kentucky, there could have been no disunion and no coercion.   Certainly, Abraham Lincoln, though born a Kentuckian, did not possess Kentucky eyes.

Kentucky wanted above all else to preserve the Union and the peace between the North and the South.   If there were good and sufficient reasons why Kentucky opposed civil war, there were also a number of excellent reasons why Kentucky opposed the dissolution of the Union.   Disunion was for Kentucky the greatests of evils and a remedy for none.   Any scheme by which she was to surrender an enviable position in the very heart of a great and prosperous nation had to have some compensating benefits.   All that Kentucky felt she would gain by joining a southern confederacy was that she would get rid of associating under the same government with people " who did not admire negro slavery and had the ill manners or the impudence to say so." [1]   She was far enough north to realize that the North had not been abolitionized and that Lincoln would be powerless to interfere with slavery (except in case of civil war) even if he wished to do so, because the sentiment of the North was then overwhelmingly conservative.

The slaveholding interests in Kentucky had nothing to gain by a disunion on the line of the Ohio River.   If Kentucky united herself with the South there was only the shadow of security for the institution of slavery in her territory even should there be no civil war.   For disunion on the slave line meant bringing Canada down to the Ohio River.   It was hardly to be expected that the free states would return any fugitive slaves in the event of Kentucky's secession and as Prentice said, breaking up the Union to preserve slavery in Kentucky was like breaking down stable doors to keep horses from running away.   On the other hand, disunion on any line south of Kentucky would cut her off from the free navigation of the Mississippi River.   If the mouth of that river were in the hands of a foreign government, the economic interests of Kentucky would be sure to suffer irreparably.

The Kentuckians of that day were accused of lacking in sectional sympathy with the slaveholding South.   However, it should be recalled that the Kentuckians of that generation had been trained in the school of the great nationalist, Henry Clay, and as one of them said, they felt that they owed no fealty to any section, "which was not in strict subordination to the higher, nobler, worthier fealty which

---

[1] Some of the northerners of 1860 may have considered slavery a question of morals, but it was not so regarded in the South. To a southerner, the northern abuse of the slave system was a breach of good manners tinged with hypocrisy. The southerners considered Charles Sumner's manners as barbarous as Charles Sumner considered the slave system.

they owed to their country—that is to the whole nation. But if there was any section above all others, of which they were bound in close sympathy by the ties of friendship and permanent interest, it was their own section—that of which they were the heart and center, the great valley of the Mississippi.[1]   The manifest destiny of the states of the Mississippi Valley was that they should remain one and inseparable (and the Mississippi was understood to include its tributaries).   This great river system was "a bond of union made by nature herself" and the Kentuckians thought that union should be maintained forever.

It should carefully be borne in mind by all of those who wish to understand the position of Kentucky at this time that her people regarded both the action of the South Carolians and that of the Black Republicans as precipitate.   If the South Carolinians were the "red precipitates," the stiff-necked Lincoln was a "black precipitate."   However, the stirring strains of the southern call "Aux armes, citoyens, formez vos bataillons," was heard with more sympathy in Kentucky than was Lincoln's call for troops.[2]   The Kentucky governor's reply to the Lincoln requisition was to the effect that Kentucky would furnish no troops for the wicked purpose of subjugating her sister states.   Nevertheless a majority of the Kentuckians were more or less enraged at

[1] S. S. Nicholas's *Essays, Conservative and Legal*, pp. 138, 139.

[2] The resolutions adopted at a Unionist meeting endorsed the Governor's response to Lincoln's requisition for troops.   See the *Louisville Journal*, April 17, 1861, and also April 16, 1861, as follows: "We understand an impression prevails in some quarters that the President's most extraordinary and unjustifiable Proclamation is illegal.   This impression is not correct.   The Proclamation is strictly within the letter of the law.   The legality of the Proclamation is its only redeeming feature, and this feature doesn't redeem it.   Far otherwise."   Of course, if the Unionist *Journal* endorsed the refusal to send troops, the southern press and party also endorsed it.

South Carolina's action. To say the least they regarded is as a great tactical blunder.

The border states were not secessionist *per se* and, therefore had very little sympathy with South Carolina. It doubtless seemed to them that South Carolina never lost an opportunity to raise the flag of disunion or the red banner of revolution. Just after the John Brown raid into Virginia in the fall of 1859, South Carolina had sent Memminger as an ambassador to the other slaveholding states to unify them against the aggressions of the Black Republicans. The border states men seem to have felt that it was a case of "incipient secession" on the part of South Carolina. Brown's raid into Virginia had deeply excited the South, where it was widely felt that the author of the House Divided speech and the Irrepressible Conflict oration had plowed the ground for such outrages, and of course, such outrages plowed the ground for secession. But, as soon as A. H. H. Stuart of Virginia perceived the significance of South Carolina's messenger, he wrote Crittenden of Kentucky: "For God's sake, give us a rallying point. Memminger is here." [1] As a result, the old Whigs of the border slave states launched the Constitutional Unionist Party. They were the "Union Savers" *par excellence*. At the first signs of danger to the perpetuity of the Union, the border states and especially Kentucky, came forward and stood to the last between the extremes of the North and the South like "the prophet of old between the living and the dead to stay the pestilence." In this region, it was understood that the secession threats were made in ernest.

During this time Kentucky was afflicted with too many leaders and was distracted with divided counsels in regard to

[1] Crittenden papers, Stuart to Crittenden, Jan. 22, 1860. See *Louisville Courier*, Jan. 31, 1860, for Memminger's speech before the Virginia Legislature.

the best policy to gain her ends. Henry Clay was dead and it seemed that "Ulysses had gone upon his wanderings and there was none left in all Ithaca who could bend his bow." Perhaps the Kentuckian of that day who was best equipped to inherit the mantle of Henry Clay was John C. Breckinridge, Vice-President of the United States under Buchanan, Senator-elect from Kentucky to succeed the venerable Crittenden at the expiration of his term, and candidate of the southern Democrats for the presidency in 1860. Breckinridge is said to have possessed like Clay "a charming personality" and was gifted with brilliancy. In 1861, Breckinridge advocated the secession of Kentucky and of all the slave states in order to reconstruct the Union and annihilate the northern sectional dictation of national policy. From within the ranks of the Democratic party in Kentucky, Breckinridge's policy was opposed by James Guthrie of Louisville. Nobody in Louisville seems to have liked any policy which they thought took chances on both the Union and civil war.[1] George D. Prentice, the great Whig editor of the *Louisville Journal,* opposed this policy. John J. Crittenden was also in opposition to it. None of them thought that the condition existing in 1861 required such extreme medicine.

However, on some points the Kentucky leaders were at one. Upon the secession of South Carolina, Crittenden introduced the so-called Crittenden Compromise, which it seems had been prepared by Madison Johnson of Lexington, Ky., in consultation with Guthrie, Breckinridge and Crittenden.[2] This proposition proved acceptable to everybody but the Republican party leaders and the radical minority. It was not only defeated in the Senate by the Republicans but was

---

[1] This does not mean that there were no Breckinridge men in Louisville.

[2] Crittenden papers, Dec., 1860.

prevented by them from being referred to the American people for acceptance or rejection before the controversy was pushed to the bloody extreme. Cassius M. Clay,[1] one of the leading Kentucky Republicans of that day, in fact, practically all of the Kentuckians, with the exception of Abraham Lincoln whom some have considered a product of Kentucky, favored adjustment rather than civil war or a dissolution of the Union.

After the failure of the Crittenden Compromise, Kentuckians refused to consider it an ultimatum. They seemed to have felt that if an earthquake should swallow up the state it would not be more disastrous to them than disunion and civil war. They, therefore, responded with alacrity to the Virginia summons for a Peace Conference. Unfortunately, the delegations from the northern states were made up of carefully picked " not-an-inch " Republicans, and the Peace Conference made no headway toward conciliation.[2] It so happened that neither the Peace Conference delegations nor the members of the United States Congress were freshly elected by the people on the issue of " compromise and peace " *versus* " civil war before compromise." And the predominant groups of leaders in the northern states felt that the efforts at compromise were nothing

---

[1] Chase papers, Clay to Chase, Feb. 1, 1861.

[2] James B. Clay reported that he found at the Peace Conference " such miserable trickery, log-rolling, and clap-trap as would disgrace a county meeting to manufacture a platform for a constable to stand on." James B. Clay, one of the Kentucky commissioners to the Peace Conference called by Virginia, was a son of Henry Clay. For James B. Clay's speech see the Kentucky *Yeoman*, March 20, 1861. See also Tyler papers, Julia Tyler to her mother, Feb. 3, 1861 : " There seems such a fixed determination to do mischief on the part of the Black Republicans." Julia Tyler was with ex-Pres. John Tyler at the Peace Conference. Tyler was the presiding officer.

but an attempt to perpetuate the power of the Democrats by ruining the Republican party.[1]

In the meantime, the Kentucky Legislature suggested the calling of a great national convention freshly elected by the American people, to deal with the subjects in controversy as became a free, intelligent and enlightened people. Kentucky did not want the Union to be broken in the "mortar of secession to be strung together on a rope of sand", but neither did she want a higher law than the Constitution of the United States as interpreted by the Supreme Court to be set up by the Republican minority. The Republicans consented to calling a National Convention, provided there was no disturbance of the public peace before they got it called.

However, the reënforcement of Fort Sumter directly brought on a so-called disturbance of the public peace and a call for 75,000 troops was thus substituted for the call of a National Convention. Of course, it was obvious after the spring elections that the non-compromising Republicans could secure only a minority of the delegates to such a Convention freshly elected by the people. Moreover, the calling of such a convention would have been a substantial admission on the part of the Republican leaders that they, themselves, were not representative of the nation and that their argument in favor of a sectional control of the national government was invalid. In other words, the calling of a National Convention would have amounted to an admission that the Republican party leaders were wrong in the premises — not on the slavery question, but on the matter of their advocacy of a sectional control of the national presidency. Lincoln's statement that if Anderson came out of Sumter, he, himself, would have to come out of the White

[1] See footnote to chapter iv, *supra*, pp. 64-66.

House[1] was doubtless a correct estimate of the effect a withdrawal of the troops from Sumter and the calling of a National Convention would have had on the political fortunes of the sectional Republican party. It can be readily understood just why Republican party politicians would prefer the reënforcing of Sumter to the calling of a National Convention. An appeal to the brain of the nation meant the party's annihilation, while an appeal to the brawn of the north meant the party's salvation. Manifestly, there was no way to save the Republican party if it made an appeal to a National Convention, that American Court of last resort, the legality of whose decisions, no mere political party has yet offered to challenge. By refraining from such an appeal, the Republican leaders violated the most fundamental of the requirements for the preservation of domestic tranquillity or peace — that greatest of the purposes for which government is instituted among men. It can do no harm to conjecture what the policy of the Republican leaders would have been, had the calling of a National Convention meant a continuation of their own political supremacy and control of the national government. The road to power is rather obviously the road they took, but, they thereby resigned all claims to a statesmanship equal to that of 1787.

After the failure of the Peace Concerence and while the Republicans were slowly gaining ground by their Fabian policy of masterly inactivity until the patience of the secessionists *per se* became exhausted, the Kentuckians busied themselves very tardily with choosing members to a border

---

[1] *Diary of a Public Man*, p. 487 (March 6) : " Well, you say Major Anderson is a good man, and I have no doubt he is ; but if he is right it will be a bad job for me if Kentucky secedes. When he goes out of Sumter [peaceful evacuation] I shall have to go out of the White House."

state convention. It seems that the purpose of this convention was to give everybody a choice between the northern and southern extremes by offering them a plan for a peaceful reconstruction of the Union which would exclude all states from membership who would not renounce the heresies of a higher law than the Constitution of the United States as interpreted by the Supreme Court and secession as one of the legal rights of a state. Massachusetts and South Carolina might have been temporarily left out of the reconstructed union and needless to say the public leaders who were committed unequivocably to the essential doctrines of these states would have been buried beyond resurrection, politically speaking.[1] The spring elections are indelible evidence[2] that one of the border states' plans would have carried if they could have gotten their propositions concretely before the American people before the veering of public opinion caused by the firing at Fort Sumter. S. S. Nicholas of Louisville fully realized the situation and Crittenden would have acted more quickly but he wanted to try all constitutional means first before resorting to unconstitutional measures.[3] The old Whigs would not follow Breckinridge, yet they could agree on nothing in this emergency which had the swift concreteness of Breckinridge's plan. Crittenden said that Henry Clay would have been worth his weight in gold many thousands of times if but once more he could have come forth from Ashland with his

---

[1] Some of the Kentuckians thought that the citizens of Massachusetts and South Carolina should be colonized somewhere together beyond the bounds of civilization and thus enable the peace to be kept in the United States.

[2] Chase papers, Nash to Chase, April 9, 1861, "The elections show that the combination of Douglas men, Americans and others voting for Lincoln last year, can be induced to unite."

[3] Crittenden papers, Crittenden to S. S. Nicholas, Dec., 1860.

irresistible eloquence and eagle glance.[1]   As it was, the Republicans were audaciously proclaiming that Lincoln stood where Clay stood.[2]

After the stirring up of Fort Sumter and the calling out of 75,000 troops, the Kentucky leaders had only a forlorn hope of either restoring peace or of preserving the union without war to the bitter end.[3]   The young men generally came to the conclusion that the only possible course was to join the confederacy, while the men over fifty came to the conclusion that the Union must be sustained at all hazards.[1]

There can be no doubt that the most intelligent Kentuckians understood that civil war meant emancipation. The southern party put great emphasis on the fact that Old Abe was craftily engineering a huge John Brown raid into the South, Joseph Holt's aunt had great difficulty in not believing that Old Abe was coming with an army of negroes to smash things up in the South even though her nephew, one of the prominent Kentucky unionists, severely assured her otherwise.[5]   It can be readily understood what a disagreeable task it was for Kentucky to take either side of the Brothers' War.   All Kentuckians were more or less like the man who sold goods to a firm in Tennessee but received no pay for his goods and who was arrested and condemned

[1] Speech of Crittenden reported in the *Louisville Journal*, March 22, 1861.

[2] *New York Tribune*, Feb. 2, 1861; *Boston Atlas and Bee*, Aug. 24, 1860; *Cincinnati Gazette*, Aug. 11, 1860; *Worcester Spy*, Oct. 10, 1860; *The Great Rebellion*, by J. M. Botts, p. 196, Lincoln's assertion "I have always been an old-line Henry Clay Whig."

[3] *Louisville Journal*, April 20, 1861, "Kentuckians! You constitute today the forlorn hope of the Union. Will you stand firm and gloriously in the breach or will you ignobly and insanely fly?"

[4] *Official Records, War of the Rebellion*, vol. iv, p. 313, Thomas to Cameron, Oct. 21, 1861.

[5] Holt papers, Mary Stephens to Joseph Holt, May, 1861.

for treason by the Lincoln government for trading with the enemy. Robbed in one confederacy and shot in the other, his ghost was grateful to neither.

Regardless of the permanent interests of Kentucky, her antipathy to the Lincoln policy almost took her out of the Union. It was possible to prevent her immediate secession only by passing a declaration of armed neutrality as the position of the state during the strife.[1]   Armed neutrality was a perfectly logical position for a people who were equally opposed to disunion and coercion. But it is not possible to say that either group of leaders in Kentucky thought that it would be a tenable position. It was a temporary expedient and was a sort of armed truce between the opposing forces in the state and nation so far as Kentucky was concerned— between those who wished to sustain the rights of the South and to sustain only an administration of the national government which was sworn to uphold the Constitution of the United States as interpreted by the Supreme Court and those who felt that the general government must be sustained at all hazards even though the administration were totally obnoxious. The great Whig editor, George D. Prentice, vividly explained to the Kentucky Unionists' satisfaction that " the office of apostle was not to be abolished because Judas was one apostle." Lincoln, the old Whig showed, was not the United States Government, and his office was brief and fleeting, while it was to be hoped that the government would last forever and the distinction would be observed between a permanent office and a temporary officer. The truce of armed neutrality was agreed to

---

[1] " Neutrality," according to Paul Shipman, associate editor of the *Louisville Journal*, "was the covering which the larva of Kentucky Unionism spun for its protection." See Paul Shipman's unpublished manuscript account of Kentucky's Neutrality for which I am indebted to John Wilson Townsend.

by both Lincoln[1] and Davis,[2] neither of whom was much
better prepared for war than were the people of Kentucky.
However, neutrality was a position of more value to the
North than to the South. The Southerners were at great disadvantage because they received no considerable help from
the Southern Confederacy. The Unionists opposed the state
arming herself because the Kentucky Governor was a southern sympathizer and consequently they feared that all the
arms purchased by the state would be turned against the
Union. The two groups of leaders agreed finally on a joint
commission composed of both groups with the commander of
the state militia holding the balance of power. This was
General Simon Bolivar Buckner,[3] who the Unionists had
reason to believe might be persuaded to side with them but

[1] Among the executive papers of Governor Magoffin is the following
memorandum signed with the initials and in the handwriting of John J.
Crittenden: "It is my duty as I conceive to suppress an insurrection
existing within the United States. I wish to do this with the least
possible disturbance or annoyance to well-disposed people anywhere.
So far I have not sent an armed force into Kentucky; nor have I any
present purpose to do so. I sincerely desire that no necessity for it
may be presented; but I mean to say nothing which shall hereafter
embarrass me in the performance of what may seem to be my duty."
This memorandum was furnished General Buckner in the presence of
John J. Crittenden. It is dated July 10, 1861, and is very typical of
President Lincoln's methods of procedure. It was not intended for
publication and therefore not signed by the wary President. For an
excellent account of the Southern Confederacy's commercial reasons
for recognizing Kentucky's neutrality, see E. Merton Coulter's "The
Effects of Secession on the Commerce of the Mississippi Valley" in
Mississippi Valley Historical Review, Dec., 1916.

[2] *Official Records*, vol. iv, pp. 190-191, Sept. 13, 1861.

[3] *Ibid.*, vol. iv, p. 255, Aug. 17, 1861. To the Honorable Secretary of
War, from A. Lincoln, "Unless there be reason to the contrary, not
known to me, make out a commission for Simon B. Buckner, of Kentucky, as a brigadier-general of volunteers. It is to be put in the hands
of General Anderson, and delivered to Gen. Buckner or not, at the discretion of Gen. Anderson. Of course, it is to remain a secret unless
and until the commission is delivered."

who afterward became a southern general. The Federal Goverment sent arms into the state to be distributed among Unionists in lieu of the guns which the young southern sympathizers were taking south with them as they went to join the Confederate armies. Some of the guns shipped in by the Federals also fell into southern hands; for there were some who did not hesitate to take the oath of allegiance to the Constitution of the United States (with the mental reservation "as interpreted by the Supreme Court") and proceed south with the arms thus secured.

The southern party was placed at an additional disadvantage which was an even greater handicap than the lack of munitions. The columns of the most powerful paper in the state, the *Louisville Journal,* were turned against the southern side. Napoleon is said to have remarked that he dreaded four hostile newspapers more than an army of 100,000 men. The circulation of the *Journal* was the largest of any paper in the entire middle section of the Union and it was doubtless equal to 40,000 men in the Union army at this time.

The editor of this paper was George D. Prentice, whose only children, two well-beloved sons, joined the Confederate army. Prentice was the intellectual match for any man in the country; his mastery of the English language, his pungent wit, his incomparable understanding of the principles of American government, conbined to make the editorials of the *Journal* tremendously effective. The following editorial will give some clue to why he proved not only a "thorn but a whole forest of thorns"[1] in the flesh of the southern party:

" Nullification is or assumes to be the right of a state to

[1] *Louisville Journal,* July 8, 1861, "Our neighbor of the *Courier* calls us the Devil. We are sorry we can't occasionally lay a gentle hand on him without him thinking that the Devil has got hold of him."

nullify Federal laws under the Constitution; it claims to be a strictly constitutional right. Revolution or the right of resistance to insufferable tyranny by whatever name it is known, makes no such absurd pretentions. It underlies all political forms and does not ask their sanction. It is the extreme medicine' of society and does not rate itself as ' daily food.' It is a forcible right, and does not demand with impunity that which belongs to a peaceable one. It carries with it openly the solemn issues of life and death and does not trip lightly forward on trivial occasions. It is the explosion of human nature under the compression of political abuses, and does not occur until the pressure has grown insupportable. In all these respects, and thousand others, it is utterly unlike nullification, which professes to be a legitimate and constitutional remedy for any mere ordinary act of the nation which a state may please to deem noxious. Nullification is the establishment of revolution as a constituent force of the government; a more pernicious heresy could hardly be conceived. Our neighbor (a southern democratic editor) is confounding it with that grand old right of resistance to oppression which no free man since the world began has ever denied. This shows that he is either writing without thinking or thinking to precious little purposes. He is puzzling the wits of his readers and cudgelling his own about a matter that is as plain as the nose on his face or as plain as his face itself." [1]

It was the Louisville Journal which first raised the white standard of neutrality even before the firing at Sumter and continued to press for this decision from the Kentucky Legislature until the neutrality resolutions were actually passed and until the southern sympathizing governor was forced to issue the neutrality preclamation toward the last

[1] *Ibid.*, March 3, 1860.

of May, 1861.[1] The Journal pointed out that secession in Kentucky would instantly make her the seat of war. And war as Prentice described it was so vivid—with the Kentucky river towns in ashes, the Kentucky fertile fields plowed by artillery wheels and the hurtling iron storm of cannon balls, the Kentucky roads resounding with the tramp of armed men and in addition, the wails of affrighted women and children, the roar of fires and the crash of falling bridges—that it is not surprising that the people of Kentucky consented to pause until the state was at least armed. Upon whom was the blow to fall most heavily, the *Journal* asked, and answered, " Upon defenseless women and children. These are the persons who suffer most in their poverty, loneliness and desolation, protracted it may be through many years. Dying on the battlefield is not the only form of suffering by any means. And yet the seceding states are anxious to precipitate all the horrors of war upon the border states and to compel us to be the shield to protect their property and their families."

" Kentucky," Prentice assured his readers, " though standing near the brink of a precipice, occupies a lofty and proud position. The path of duty which so often is arduous and painful, is for Kentucky the safe and flowery path of peace. Let Kentucky firmly maintain her position of submitting to the constitutional authority of the general government but maintaining her neutrality and protesting against war, and she will save her fields from being ravaged, impoverished and desolate, crippled in power, demoralized in character and half surrounded by enemies where undying hatred and jealousy would be the endless source of

---

[1] *Ibid.*, Jan. 28, 1861, " And when the shock of war shall, if it must come at some future day, let Kentucky be found standing in armed neutrality beneath the white flag of peace—an asylum for the victims of Civil War, and a sublime example to our erring countrymen."

renewed troubles and wars. When we calmly survey the
blessings of peace and union which Kentucky may enjoy
in contrast with the dark and bloody ruin into which she
would plunge by secession, we are tempted to ask if there is
any sane man in Kentucky who is willing for the sake of
engaging in a civil war for which there is no just cause, to
leap into this yawning gulf and drag down his family,
friends, countrymen and even liberty itself. . . . Peace is
prosperity and liberty, as war is desolation and despotism.
If Kentucky would preserve her own independence and
civil liberty from the perils of this conflict, let her stand
where she is, in peaceful neutrality."[1] So much for the
forceful ideas by the propagation of which Prentice made
possible Kentucky's temporary neutrality.

Kentucky's neutrality was not formally violated until
September, when a southern army occupied Columbus to
prevent a northern army from getting there first.[2] From a
military point of view this may have been a good move, but
politically speaking it was almost as deplorable for the
southern cause in Kentucky as the firing at Sumter was for
that cause in the northern states.[3] The Legislature which
had been elected in August and met in September requested
the southern army to withdraw, without making the same
request of the Federal troops which were being enlisted
within the state.[4] The Federal Government had taken
great care not to establish a camp in the state until after
the August elections for the State Legislature; the southern
party had hoped that the Federal Government would take
such action because it was felt that if the Kentucky people
were absolutely convinced that they would have to fight on

[1] *Louisville Journal*, May 29, 1861.
[2] *Official Records*, vol. iv, p. 181, Sept. 4, 1861.
[3] *Ibid.*, vol. iv, pp. 411-412, Sept. 18, 1861.
[4] *Ibid.*, vol. iv, pp. 411-412, Sept. 18, 1861.

one side or the other, the majority would espouse the southern cause. The Unionists had taken care to get candidates for the Legislature of an unconditional variety "without any ifs," and they apparently succeeded.[1]

However, there were men in this Legislature elected at the August elections who would have turned the state over to the Confederacy if the premature Emancipation Proclamation of General Fremont had not been promptly annulled by the Lincoln Administration. In the event that the Proclamation of 1861 had been sustained, Speed, Lincoln's right-hand man in Kentucky, felt that it would be as hopeless to hold Kentucky as it would have been to row a boat up Niagara Falls.[2] The Kentuckians were opposed to emancipation by the sword. Nor was the North ripe at this time for the revelation of this policy. The Battle of Bull Run increased the number of abolitionists tremendously, but even by the first of January, 1863, there was hardly enough backing in popular sentiment to sustain such a measure as a necessity of war. And it was with the utmost difficulty that two-thirds of Congress was finally mustered behind the Thirteenth Amendment to the Constitution, even in 1865, and three-fourths of the states could only be obtained by requiring the seceded southern states to accept this as a condition to their re-admittance to the reign of civil law.

Kentucky's Unionist decision, if it can be called a decision when so many of her sons fought in the southern army, was of the utmost importance to the Lincoln administration, because it gave some few shreds of nationalism to cover its original sectionalism—and of these shreds,

[1] Prentice wanted true union men nominated for the Legislature, "not some political tadpole who will lose his Union tail before the Legislature meets." *Louisville Journal*, July 3, 1861.

[2] Holt papers, Speed to Holt, Sept. 7, 1861.

the Republicans were sadly in need.[1] It seems that the
Lincoln administration rightly regarded the political situation in Kentucky as of more importance than the military
situation. The neutrality of the peaceable Kentuckians was
thus essentially nationalistic in its effect. In any event it
cannot be said that the Kentuckians were not willing to do
their utmost to sustain government based on consent. For
Kentucky contributed quotas to both armies [2] and fortunate
indeed was the Kentucky family whose members were all
in the same army. She had longed desperately to prevent
the interregnum of war, for she knew that peace meant
a continuation without interruption of liberty and that war
would bring despotism and desolation. Her reward was
the crown of thorns. And yet she will not have suffered in
vain if the world some day comes to understand, as she understood, how to hold the balance evenly between two extremes. " Doth not wisdom cry and understanding put
forth her voice, by me princes rule and nobles, even all the
judges of the earth."

At one of the Kentucky reunions, where the men who
wore the blue and the men who wore the grey were frater-
nally assembled together, a Union veteran was heard to
murmur that the Kentucky Confederates always spoke as if
they had won the Civil War. In a certain sense it must be
admitted that the South did win the Civil War. It should
be borne in mind that she stood primarily for the Constitution of the United States as interpreted by the Supreme
Court and that she refused to submit peacefully to a sec-

[1] Speed to his mother, Oct. 29, 1861, " I had a long talk with him
(Gen. Banks) about the future. He looks upon our action in Kentucky
as worth everything to the Government. It nationalizes the contest and
renders either compromise or peace impossible except upon terms of
submission to the national will, liberally and fairly construed."

[2] Both sides fought for the perpetuation of government based on
consent.

tional control of the national government. Her position on both of these points has been sustained, although there are no amendments in the Constitution announcing the consummation. It is true that slavery was abolished by the Civil War, but the Northerners did not fight to free the slaves. And the Civil War Amendments which the Republican Party incorporated in the Constitution of the United States at the point of the sword have not been able to touch the brain quality of the African. The position of the negro in the United States remains relatively the same; for two generations is not sufficient to modify inherited tendencies which are the result of thousands of years of past environment. It is extremely difficult for a fair-minded person to say that the Civil War Amendments did not put the cart before the horse. Moreover to assert that war was the only method by which the slaves could have been freed is, not only to deny the efficacy of popular government, but also to slander the *bona fide* abolitionists of 1860—for, in view of the economic conditions of modern times, they felt that abolition by the sword was entirely superfluous, since the slave system was even then on its economic deathbed.

When Abraham Lincoln took the decisive step which led to the " disturbance of the public peace," he evidently did so with the expectation that the public opinion of the future would forgive a civil war which resulted in the abolition of slavery. There can be no doubt that he correctly estimated the trend of public opinion even up to the present time. However, a new current has set in which he did not take into consideration. Public opinion is now turning against war—and especially against civil war, as a just and desirable method of settling disputes between civilized people. Because of this new trend of public opinion, the civilized world may yet reverse its present decision on the Civil War. It is entirely probable that the public of 1961 may hold that there need have been no appeal from the ballot to the bullet in 1861, had the American people of that day possessed sufficient political sagacity to distinguish between appearances and reality.